metrix
EST PREPARATION

I0891987

CLEP®

nformation Systems and omputer Applications Secrets Study Guide

DEAR FUTURE EXAM SUCCESS STORY

First of all, **THANK YOU** for purchasing Mometrix study materials!

Second, congratulations! You are one of the few determined test-takers who are committed to doing whatever it takes to excel on your exam. **You have come to the right place.** We developed these study materials with one goal in mind: to deliver you the information you need in a format that's concise and easy to use.

In addition to optimizing your guide for the content of the test, we've outlined our recommended steps for breaking down the preparation process into small, attainable goals so you can make sure you stay on track.

We've also analyzed the entire test-taking process, identifying the most common pitfalls and showing how you can overcome them and be ready for any curveball the test throws you.

Standardized testing is one of the biggest obstacles on your road to success, which only increases the importance of doing well in the high-pressure, high-stakes environment of test day. Your results on this test could have a significant impact on your future, and this guide provides the information and practical advice to help you achieve your full potential on test day.

Your success is our success

We would love to hear from you! If you would like to share the story of your exam success or if you have any questions or comments in regard to our products, please contact us at **800-673-8175** or **support@mometrix.com**.

Thanks again for your business and we wish you continued success!

Sincerely,
The Mometrix Test Preparation Team

Written and edited by the Mometrix Exam Secrets Test Prep Team
Printed in the United States of America

TABLE OF CONTENTS

Introduction

Thank you for purchasing this resource! You have made the choice to prepare yourself for a test that could have a huge impact on your future, and this guide is designed to help you be fully ready for test day. Obviously, it's important to have a solid understanding of the test material, but you also need to be prepared for the unique environment and stressors of the test, so that you can perform to the best of your abilities.

For this purpose, the first section that appears in this guide is the **Secret Keys**. We've devoted countless hours to meticulously researching what works and what doesn't, and we've boiled down our findings to the five most impactful steps you can take to improve your performance on the test. We start at the beginning with study planning and move through the preparation process, all the way to the testing strategies that will help you get the most out of what you know when you're finally sitting in front of the test.

We recommend that you start preparing for your test as far in advance as possible. However, if you've bought this guide as a last-minute study resource and only have a few days before your test, we recommend that you skip over the first two Secret Keys since they address a long-term study plan.

If you struggle with **test anxiety**, we strongly encourage you to check out our recommendations for how you can overcome it. Test anxiety is a formidable foe, but it can be beaten, and we want to make sure you have the tools you need to defeat it.

Secret Key #1 – Plan Big, Study Small

There's a lot riding on your performance. If you want to ace this test, you're going to need to keep your skills sharp and the material fresh in your mind. You need a plan that lets you review everything you need to know while still fitting in your schedule. We'll break this strategy down into three categories.

Information Organization

Start with the information you already have: the official test outline. From this, you can make a complete list of all the concepts you need to cover before the test. Organize these concepts into groups that can be studied together, and create a list of any related vocabulary you need to learn so you can brush up on any difficult terms. You'll want to keep this vocabulary list handy once you actually start studying since you may need to add to it along the way.

Time Management

Once you have your set of study concepts, decide how to spread them out over the time you have left before the test. Break your study plan into small, clear goals so you have a manageable task for each day and know exactly what you're doing. Then just focus on one small step at a time. When you manage your time this way, you don't need to spend hours at a time studying. Studying a small block of content for a short period each day helps you retain information better and avoid stressing over how much you have left to do. You can relax knowing that you have a plan to cover everything in time. In order for this strategy to be effective though, you have to start studying early and stick to your schedule. Avoid the exhaustion and futility that comes from last-minute cramming!

Study Environment

The environment you study in has a big impact on your learning. Studying in a coffee shop, while probably more enjoyable, is not likely to be as fruitful as studying in a quiet room. It's important to keep distractions to a minimum. You're only planning to study for a short block of time, so make the most of it. Don't pause to check your phone or get up to find a snack. It's also important to **avoid multitasking**. Research has consistently shown that multitasking will make your studying dramatically less effective. Your study area should also be comfortable and well-lit so you don't have the distraction of straining your eyes or sitting on an uncomfortable chair.

The time of day you study is also important. You want to be rested and alert. Don't wait until just before bedtime. Study when you'll be most likely to comprehend and remember. Even better, if you know what time of day your test will be, set that time aside for study. That way your brain will be used to working on that subject at that specific time and you'll have a better chance of recalling information.

Finally, it can be helpful to team up with others who are studying for the same test. Your actual studying should be done in as isolated an environment as possible, but the work of organizing the information and setting up the study plan can be divided up. In between study sessions, you can discuss with your teammates the concepts that you're all studying and quiz each other on the details. Just be sure that your teammates are as serious about the test as you are. If you find that your study time is being replaced with social time, you might need to find a new team.

Secret Key #2 – Make Your Studying Count

You're devoting a lot of time and effort to preparing for this test, so you want to be absolutely certain it will pay off. This means doing more than just reading the content and hoping you can remember it on test day. It's important to make every minute of study count. There are two main areas you can focus on to make your studying count.

Retention

It doesn't matter how much time you study if you can't remember the material. You need to make sure you are retaining the concepts. To check your retention of the information you're learning, try recalling it at later times with minimal prompting. Try carrying around flashcards and glance at one or two from time to time or ask a friend who's also studying for the test to quiz you.

To enhance your retention, look for ways to put the information into practice so that you can apply it rather than simply recalling it. If you're using the information in practical ways, it will be much easier to remember. Similarly, it helps to solidify a concept in your mind if you're not only reading it to yourself but also explaining it to someone else. Ask a friend to let you teach them about a concept you're a little shaky on (or speak aloud to an imaginary audience if necessary). As you try to summarize, define, give examples, and answer your friend's questions, you'll understand the concepts better and they will stay with you longer. Finally, step back for a big picture view and ask yourself how each piece of information fits with the whole subject. When you link the different concepts together and see them working together as a whole, it's easier to remember the individual components.

Finally, practice showing your work on any multi-step problems, even if you're just studying. Writing out each step you take to solve a problem will help solidify the process in your mind, and you'll be more likely to remember it during the test.

Modality

Modality simply refers to the means or method by which you study. Choosing a study modality that fits your own individual learning style is crucial. No two people learn best in exactly the same way, so it's important to know your strengths and use them to your advantage.

For example, if you learn best by visualization, focus on visualizing a concept in your mind and draw an image or a diagram. Try color-coding your notes, illustrating them, or creating symbols that will trigger your mind to recall a learned concept. If you learn best by hearing or discussing information, find a study partner who learns the same way or read aloud to yourself. Think about how to put the information in your own words. Imagine that you are giving a lecture on the topic and record yourself so you can listen to it later.

For any learning style, flashcards can be helpful. Organize the information so you can take advantage of spare moments to review. Underline key words or phrases. Use different colors for different categories. Mnemonic devices (such as creating a short list in which every item starts with the same letter) can also help with retention. Find what works best for you and use it to store the information in your mind most effectively and easily.

Secret Key #3 – Practice the Right Way

Your success on test day depends not only on how many hours you put into preparing, but also on whether you prepared the right way. It's good to check along the way to see if your studying is paying off. One of the most effective ways to do this is by taking practice tests to evaluate your progress. Practice tests are useful because they show exactly where you need to improve. Every time you take a practice test, pay special attention to these three groups of questions:

- The questions you got wrong
- The questions you had to guess on, even if you guessed right
- The questions you found difficult or slow to work through

This will show you exactly what your weak areas are, and where you need to devote more study time. Ask yourself why each of these questions gave you trouble. Was it because you didn't understand the material? Was it because you didn't remember the vocabulary? Do you need more repetitions on this type of question to build speed and confidence? Dig into those questions and figure out how you can strengthen your weak areas as you go back to review the material.

Additionally, many practice tests have a section explaining the answer choices. It can be tempting to read the explanation and think that you now have a good understanding of the concept. However, an explanation likely only covers part of the question's broader context. Even if the explanation makes perfect sense, **go back and investigate** every concept related to the question until you're positive you have a thorough understanding.

As you go along, keep in mind that the practice test is just that: practice. Memorizing these questions and answers will not be very helpful on the actual test because it is unlikely to have any of the same exact questions. If you only know the right answers to the sample questions, you won't be prepared for the real thing. **Study the concepts** until you understand them fully, and then you'll be able to answer any question that shows up on the test.

It's important to wait on the practice tests until you're ready. If you take a test on your first day of study, you may be overwhelmed by the amount of material covered and how much you need to learn. Work up to it gradually.

On test day, you'll need to be prepared for answering questions, managing your time, and using the test-taking strategies you've learned. It's a lot to balance, like a mental marathon that will have a big impact on your future. Like training for a marathon, you'll need to start slowly and work your way up. When test day arrives, you'll be ready.

Start with the strategies you've read in the first two Secret Keys—plan your course and study in the way that works best for you. If you have time, consider using multiple study resources to get different approaches to the same concepts. It can be helpful to see difficult concepts from more than one angle. Then find a good source for practice tests. Many times, the test website will suggest potential study resources or provide sample tests.

Practice Test Strategy

If you're able to find at least three practice tests, we recommend this strategy:

UNTIMED AND OPEN-BOOK PRACTICE

Take the first test with no time constraints and with your notes and study guide handy. Take your time and focus on applying the strategies you've learned.

TIMED AND OPEN-BOOK PRACTICE

Take the second practice test open-book as well, but set a timer and practice pacing yourself to finish in time.

TIMED AND CLOSED-BOOK PRACTICE

Take any other practice tests as if it were test day. Set a timer and put away your study materials. Sit at a table or desk in a quiet room, imagine yourself at the testing center, and answer questions as quickly and accurately as possible.

Keep repeating timed and closed-book tests on a regular basis until you run out of practice tests or it's time for the actual test. Your mind will be ready for the schedule and stress of test day, and you'll be able to focus on recalling the material you've learned.

Secret Key #4 – Pace Yourself

Once you're fully prepared for the material on the test, your biggest challenge on test day will be managing your time. Just knowing that the clock is ticking can make you panic even if you have plenty of time left. Work on pacing yourself so you can build confidence against the time constraints of the exam. Pacing is a difficult skill to master, especially in a high-pressure environment, so **practice is vital.**

Set time expectations for your pace based on how much time is available. For example, if a section has 60 questions and the time limit is 30 minutes, you know you have to average 30 seconds or less per question in order to answer them all. Although 30 seconds is the hard limit, set 25 seconds per question as your goal, so you reserve extra time to spend on harder questions. When you budget extra time for the harder questions, you no longer have any reason to stress when those questions take longer to answer.

Don't let this time expectation distract you from working through the test at a calm, steady pace, but keep it in mind so you don't spend too much time on any one question. Recognize that taking extra time on one question you don't understand may keep you from answering two that you do understand later in the test. If your time limit for a question is up and you're still not sure of the answer, mark it and move on, and come back to it later if the time and the test format allow. If the testing format doesn't allow you to return to earlier questions, just make an educated guess; then put it out of your mind and move on.

On the easier questions, be careful not to rush. It may seem wise to hurry through them so you have more time for the challenging ones, but it's not worth missing one if you know the concept and just didn't take the time to read the question fully. Work efficiently but make sure you understand the question and have looked at all of the answer choices, since more than one may seem right at first.

Even if you're paying attention to the time, you may find yourself a little behind at some point. You should speed up to get back on track, but do so wisely. Don't panic; just take a few seconds less on each question until you're caught up. Don't guess without thinking, but do look through the answer choices and eliminate any you know are wrong. If you can get down to two choices, it is often worthwhile to guess from those. Once you've chosen an answer, move on and don't dwell on any that you skipped or had to hurry through. If a question was taking too long, chances are it was one of the harder ones, so you weren't as likely to get it right anyway.

On the other hand, if you find yourself getting ahead of schedule, it may be beneficial to slow down a little. The more quickly you work, the more likely you are to make a careless mistake that will affect your score. You've budgeted time for each question, so don't be afraid to spend that time. Practice an efficient but careful pace to get the most out of the time you have.

Secret Key #5 – Have a Plan for Guessing

When you're taking the test, you may find yourself stuck on a question. Some of the answer choices seem better than others, but you don't see the one answer choice that is obviously correct. What do you do?

The scenario described above is very common, yet most test takers have not effectively prepared for it. Developing and practicing a plan for guessing may be one of the single most effective uses of your time as you get ready for the exam.

In developing your plan for guessing, there are three questions to address:

- When should you start the guessing process?
- How should you narrow down the choices?
- Which answer should you choose?

When to Start the Guessing Process

Unless your plan for guessing is to select C every time (which, despite its merits, is not what we recommend), you need to leave yourself enough time to apply your answer elimination strategies. Since you have a limited amount of time for each question, that means that if you're going to give yourself the best shot at guessing correctly, you have to decide quickly whether or not you will guess.

Of course, the best-case scenario is that you don't have to guess at all, so first, see if you can answer the question based on your knowledge of the subject and basic reasoning skills. Focus on the key words in the question and try to jog your memory of related topics. Give yourself a chance to bring the knowledge to mind, but once you realize that you don't have (or you can't access) the knowledge you need to answer the question, it's time to start the guessing process.

It's almost always better to start the guessing process too early than too late. It only takes a few seconds to remember something and answer the question from knowledge. Carefully eliminating wrong answer choices takes longer. Plus, going through the process of eliminating answer choices can actually help jog your memory.

Summary: Start the guessing process as soon as you decide that you can't answer the question based on your knowledge.

How to Narrow Down the Choices

The next chapter in this book (**Test-Taking Strategies**) includes a wide range of strategies for how to approach questions and how to look for answer choices to eliminate. You will definitely want to read those carefully, practice them, and figure out which ones work best for you. Here though, we're going to address a mindset rather than a particular strategy.

Your odds of guessing an answer correctly depend on how many options you are choosing from.

Number of options left	5	4	3	2	1
Odds of guessing correctly	20%	25%	33%	50%	100%

You can see from this chart just how valuable it is to be able to eliminate incorrect answers and make an educated guess, but there are two things that many test takers do that cause them to miss out on the benefits of guessing:

- Accidentally eliminating the correct answer
- Selecting an answer based on an impression

We'll look at the first one here, and the second one in the next section.

To avoid accidentally eliminating the correct answer, we recommend a thought exercise called **the $5 challenge**. In this challenge, you only eliminate an answer choice from contention if you are willing to bet $5 on it being wrong. Why $5? Five dollars is a small but not insignificant amount of money. It's an amount you could afford to lose but wouldn't want to throw away. And while losing $5 once might not hurt too much, doing it twenty times will set you back $100. In the same way, each small decision you make—eliminating a choice here, guessing on a question there—won't by itself impact your score very much, but when you put them all together, they can make a big difference. By holding each answer choice elimination decision to a higher standard, you can reduce the risk of accidentally eliminating the correct answer.

The $5 challenge can also be applied in a positive sense: If you are willing to bet $5 that an answer choice *is* correct, go ahead and mark it as correct.

Summary: Only eliminate an answer choice if you are willing to bet $5 that it is wrong.

Which Answer to Choose

You're taking the test. You've run into a hard question and decided you'll have to guess. You've eliminated all the answer choices you're willing to bet $5 on. Now you have to pick an answer. Why do we even need to talk about this? Why can't you just pick whichever one you feel like when the time comes?

The answer to these questions is that if you don't come into the test with a plan, you'll rely on your impression to select an answer choice, and if you do that, you risk falling into a trap. The test writers know that everyone who takes their test will be guessing on some of the questions, so they intentionally write wrong answer choices to seem plausible. You still have to pick an answer though, and if the wrong answer choices are designed to look right, how can you ever be sure that you're not falling for their trap? The best solution we've found to this dilemma is to take the decision out of your hands entirely. Here is the process we recommend:

Once you've eliminated any choices that you are confident (willing to bet $5) are wrong, select the first remaining choice as your answer.

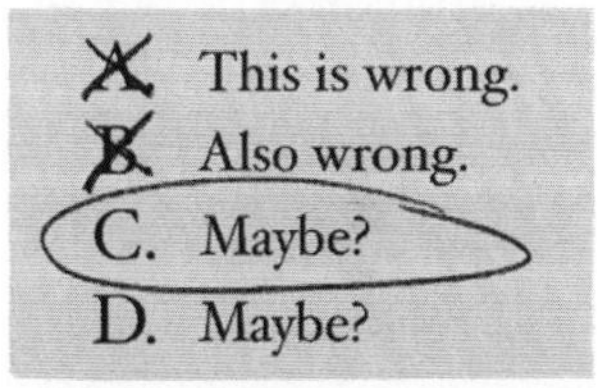

Whether you choose to select the first remaining choice, the second, or the last, the important thing is that you use some preselected standard. Using this approach guarantees that you will not be enticed into selecting an answer choice that looks right, because you are not basing your decision on how the answer choices look.

This is not meant to make you question your knowledge. Instead, it is to help you recognize the difference between your knowledge and your impressions. There's a huge difference between thinking an answer is right because of what you know, and thinking an answer is right because it looks or sounds like it should be right.

Summary: To ensure that your selection is appropriately random, make a predetermined selection from among all answer choices you have not eliminated.

Test-Taking Strategies

This section contains a list of test-taking strategies that you may find helpful as you work through the test. By taking what you know and applying logical thought, you can maximize your chances of answering any question correctly!

It is very important to realize that every question is different and every person is different: no single strategy will work on every question, and no single strategy will work for every person. That's why we've included all of them here, so you can try them out and determine which ones work best for different types of questions and which ones work best for you.

Question Strategies

✓ Read Carefully

Read the question and the answer choices carefully. Don't miss the question because you misread the terms. You have plenty of time to read each question thoroughly and make sure you understand what is being asked. Yet a happy medium must be attained, so don't waste too much time. You must read carefully and efficiently.

✓ Contextual Clues

Look for contextual clues. If the question includes a word you are not familiar with, look at the immediate context for some indication of what the word might mean. Contextual clues can often give you all the information you need to decipher the meaning of an unfamiliar word. Even if you can't determine the meaning, you may be able to narrow down the possibilities enough to make a solid guess at the answer to the question.

✓ Prefixes

If you're having trouble with a word in the question or answer choices, try dissecting it. Take advantage of every clue that the word might include. Prefixes can be a huge help. Usually, they allow you to determine a basic meaning. *Pre-* means before, *post-* means after, *pro-* is positive, *de-* is negative. From prefixes, you can get an idea of the general meaning of the word and try to put it into context.

✓ Hedge Words

Watch out for critical hedge words, such as *likely, may, can, often, almost, mostly, usually, generally, rarely*, and *sometimes*. Question writers insert these hedge phrases to cover every possibility. Often an answer choice will be wrong simply because it leaves no room for exception. Be on guard for answer choices that have definitive words such as *exactly* and *always*.

✓ Switchback Words

Stay alert for *switchbacks*. These are the words and phrases frequently used to alert you to shifts in thought. The most common switchback words are *but, although*, and *however*. Others include *nevertheless, on the other hand, even though, while, in spite of, despite*, and *regardless of*. Switchback words are important to catch because they can change the direction of the question or an answer choice.

⊘ Face Value

When in doubt, use common sense. Accept the situation in the problem at face value. Don't read too much into it. These problems will not require you to make wild assumptions. If you have to go beyond creativity and warp time or space in order to have an answer choice fit the question, then you should move on and consider the other answer choices. These are normal problems rooted in reality. The applicable relationship or explanation may not be readily apparent, but it is there for you to figure out. Use your common sense to interpret anything that isn't clear.

Answer Choice Strategies

⊘ Answer Selection

The most thorough way to pick an answer choice is to identify and eliminate wrong answers until only one is left, then confirm it is the correct answer. Sometimes an answer choice may immediately seem right, but be careful. The test writers will usually put more than one reasonable answer choice on each question, so take a second to read all of them and make sure that the other choices are not equally obvious. As long as you have time left, it is better to read every answer choice than to pick the first one that looks right without checking the others.

⊘ Answer Choice Families

An answer choice family consists of two (in rare cases, three) answer choices that are very similar in construction and cannot all be true at the same time. If you see two answer choices that are direct opposites or parallels, one of them is usually the correct answer. For instance, if one answer choice says that quantity *x* increases and another either says that quantity *x* decreases (opposite) or says that quantity *y* increases (parallel), then those answer choices would fall into the same family. An answer choice that doesn't match the construction of the answer choice family is more likely to be incorrect. Most questions will not have answer choice families, but when they do appear, you should be prepared to recognize them.

⊘ Eliminate Answers

Eliminate answer choices as soon as you realize they are wrong, but make sure you consider all possibilities. If you are eliminating answer choices and realize that the last one you are left with is also wrong, don't panic. Start over and consider each choice again. There may be something you missed the first time that you will realize on the second pass.

⊘ Avoid Fact Traps

Don't be distracted by an answer choice that is factually true but doesn't answer the question. You are looking for the choice that answers the question. Stay focused on what the question is asking for so you don't accidentally pick an answer that is true but incorrect. Always go back to the question and make sure the answer choice you've selected actually answers the question and is not merely a true statement.

⊘ Extreme Statements

In general, you should avoid answers that put forth extreme actions as standard practice or proclaim controversial ideas as established fact. An answer choice that states the "process should be used in certain situations, if…" is much more likely to be correct than one that states the "process should be discontinued completely." The first is a calm rational statement and doesn't even make a definitive, uncompromising stance, using a hedge word *if* to provide wiggle room, whereas the second choice is far more extreme.

☑ Benchmark

As you read through the answer choices and you come across one that seems to answer the question well, mentally select that answer choice. This is not your final answer, but it's the one that will help you evaluate the other answer choices. The one that you selected is your benchmark or standard for judging each of the other answer choices. Every other answer choice must be compared to your benchmark. That choice is correct until proven otherwise by another answer choice beating it. If you find a better answer, then that one becomes your new benchmark. Once you've decided that no other choice answers the question as well as your benchmark, you have your final answer.

☑ Predict the Answer

Before you even start looking at the answer choices, it is often best to try to predict the answer. When you come up with the answer on your own, it is easier to avoid distractions and traps because you will know exactly what to look for. The right answer choice is unlikely to be word-for-word what you came up with, but it should be a close match. Even if you are confident that you have the right answer, you should still take the time to read each option before moving on.

General Strategies

☑ Tough Questions

If you are stumped on a problem or it appears too hard or too difficult, don't waste time. Move on! Remember though, if you can quickly check for obviously incorrect answer choices, your chances of guessing correctly are greatly improved. Before you completely give up, at least try to knock out a couple of possible answers. Eliminate what you can and then guess at the remaining answer choices before moving on.

☑ Check Your Work

Since you will probably not know every term listed and the answer to every question, it is important that you get credit for the ones that you do know. Don't miss any questions through careless mistakes. If at all possible, try to take a second to look back over your answer selection and make sure you've selected the correct answer choice and haven't made a costly careless mistake (such as marking an answer choice that you didn't mean to mark). This quick double check should more than pay for itself in caught mistakes for the time it costs.

☑ Pace Yourself

It's easy to be overwhelmed when you're looking at a page full of questions; your mind is confused and full of random thoughts, and the clock is ticking down faster than you would like. Calm down and maintain the pace that you have set for yourself. Especially as you get down to the last few minutes of the test, don't let the small numbers on the clock make you panic. As long as you are on track by monitoring your pace, you are guaranteed to have time for each question.

☑ Don't Rush

It is very easy to make errors when you are in a hurry. Maintaining a fast pace in answering questions is pointless if it makes you miss questions that you would have gotten right otherwise. Test writers like to include distracting information and wrong answers that seem right. Taking a little extra time to avoid careless mistakes can make all the difference in your test score. Find a pace that allows you to be confident in the answers that you select.

⊘ KEEP MOVING

Panicking will not help you pass the test, so do your best to stay calm and keep moving. Taking deep breaths and going through the answer elimination steps you practiced can help to break through a stress barrier and keep your pace.

Final Notes

The combination of a solid foundation of content knowledge and the confidence that comes from practicing your plan for applying that knowledge is the key to maximizing your performance on test day. As your foundation of content knowledge is built up and strengthened, you'll find that the strategies included in this chapter become more and more effective in helping you quickly sift through the distractions and traps of the test to isolate the correct answer.

Now that you're preparing to move forward into the test content chapters of this book, be sure to keep your goal in mind. As you read, think about how you will be able to apply this information on the test. If you've already seen sample questions for the test and you have an idea of the question format and style, try to come up with questions of your own that you can answer based on what you're reading. This will give you valuable practice applying your knowledge in the same ways you can expect to on test day.

Good luck and good studying!

Business, Social, and Ethical Implications and Issues

Security Controls for Information Systems

Security controls for information systems have three different categories:

- Information system controls – make certain the information generated by the computer system is accurate. These controls work to prevent GIGO, or garbage in/garbage out—i.e., if invalid data is input into a computer, it will output invalid data. By following the audit trail, a computer can trace the entire history of a transaction and discover errors.
- Procedural controls – provide maximum security for the information system by regulating operations. This is done through separation of duties, which limits access to the information system so that a single person cannot corrupt it, and standardized procedures, which prevent errors and fraud through uniformity.
- Physical facility controls – safeguard the actual facility against physical damage, such as natural disasters.

Information System Controls

Error checking occurs when the control system checks the keyed inputs to ensure that they fall within an acceptable range of values.

Drop-down input boxes restrict the values that can be entered into the computer and, thereby, prevent invalid data.

Encryption involves altering transmitted data into an unreadable form. Before data is encrypted, it is described as plaintext. After it is encrypted, it is described as ciphertext. When encrypting the transmission, most systems use the data encryption standard, or DES, which uses different keys to encrypt and decrypt data. Decryption occurs when the transmission is restored to its initial, readable form. In public key encryption, there is the public key, which broadcasts the transmission, and a private key, which decrypts the transmission and is known only to the data receiver. The Rivest-Shamir-Adleman, or RSA, encryption is the most prevalent public key encryption method. It relies on a digital signature to verify the sender's identity.

Procedural Controls

Authentication requires users to verify their identities before they can gain access to a computer system. Only authorized users can use the system. Identity verification requires a user to input the correct password, which is a string of letters, numbers and/or symbols that are known only to the user and the system. Systems that require passwords are known as password protected. A hacker is an unauthorized user who has managed to access the system.

Biometric controls verify user identity by scanning and matching physical features, such as retinas, fingerprints or faces.

Firewalls are a procedural control designed for networks. They prevent unauthorized users for accessing the network through the Internet.

Physical Facility Controls

A Disaster recovery plan explains the tasks and responsibilities which must be fulfilled in the event of a natural disaster, such as a flood, storm, fire, etc. These plans are necessary to keep operations going; therefore, every organization should have one.

A System recovery plan explains the tasks and responsibilities that must be fulfilled when the information processing system fails. These plans can keep an organization running in the absence of computer processing, and should not be confused with a disaster recovery plan.

Certain systems are necessary to protect structures, such as buildings and plants, from physical damage. These systems include smoke detectors, fire suppression, emergency power, coolant systems, temperature controls, and humidity controls.

Malicious Programs

A virus is a type of malicious program. It attacks a computer system by first embedding itself within another program used by the system and then activating when the program is run. Viruses can be transmitted through networks (such as the Internet) and electronic mail, and can duplicate and spread into other programs. Personal computers are often susceptible to virus infections.

A worm is a type of virus. It seeks out and corrupts specific data files. It can also travel through networks and E-mail, even without user intervention.

A Trojan horse is a malicious program that performs useful tasks in the computer; however, it also contains code that collects or destroys important data after it is installed, or even allows remote access of one's computer.

Virus-checking software protects against malicious programs. It detects infection within a computer system, and eliminates the virus.

Security Protocols Used By Organizations

Using network security protocols, organizations can safeguard their information against system failures and malicious programs. Additionally, these protocols are often required by various local and federal laws and industry standards. In most cases, a network security system attempts to control access through the network nodes. It allows only authenticated users and devices to access the network, and prevents them from performing any functions that have not been authorized.

There are two popular methods of regulating access:

- Verification – uses a password or some other method to ensure that only authenticated users and devices are accessing the network.
- Firewalls – protect networks that are linked to other networks, such as the Internet. Firewalls inspect information traveling into and out of the network, and prevent suspicious activity from accessing it.

Information Processing Careers

Chief information officer, or CIO, is the executive director with the most power in overseeing information technology and computer systems within an organization. He or she usually answers to the chief executive officer, chief financial officer, or chief operations officer.

Operations managers ensure the efficient physical operation of computer equipment.

Computer operators manage the daily activity performed using computers. They make certain the computers are operating correctly and secured physically, and assist network managers and programmers. They are also responsible for logging events, such as malfunctions and the use of backup systems.

A Network manager oversees the computer network by maintaining the hardware and software that comprises it.

A Network specialist, also known as a network engineer, establishes and ensures the proper operation of the computer network.

A Programming manager oversees all programming functions and activities.

An Analyst oversees certain phases of software development, namely the analysis phase and, in some cases, the design phase. Specifically, analysts are responsible for researching IT problems, devising and recommending software and systems solutions to meet those problems, and guiding system development so that it addresses business needs.

A Database administrator, or DBA, is responsible for defining, maintaining, and ensuring the security of an organization's database and its data dictionary. Specifically, DBAs create and implement database strategies, monitor database performance, suggest ways of improvement, and plan for future additions and revisions to the database.

A Programmer helps develop and write the software that will run a system. This includes converting the design specification into code, testing the software, debugging the software, and documenting all the components that comprise the system. Programmers often specialize in a specific programming language, such as C++, Java, Lisp, PERL, etc. Programmers are also known as software engineers, software developers, software analysts and computer scientists. There are different programmers for each type of system.

An Applications programmer develops and writes programs related to information systems or applications.

A Systems programmer writes and/or maintains computer operating systems.

A Database programmer develops and creates interfaces that allow users to access and work with the database management system.

Economic Impact of Information Systems

New developments in information system technology have generally had positive economic impacts for business. This is especially true with online e-commerce, which has greatly expanded the number of people to which businesses can market and sell their products. In short, information systems have increased business profitability overall, more than offsetting the costs and investment expenditures required to develop these new systems and technologies. Unfortunately, information systems have not always been a boon to individual workers. In many cases, new technologies have automated functions normally performed by human workers and, as a consequence, put people out of work. Furthermore, workers often require additional knowledge to work with information systems. This raises the skill and education level necessary to earn a living.

Privacy Concerns

Modern information systems, such as databases, often contain large quantities of vital and sensitive information regarding individual people. As these systems become more prevalent and this information becomes more readily available, concerns over privacy arise. A person or organization can acquire sensitive information on many people simply by linking to these databases or mining data warehouses (either legally or illegally). According to the American Civil Liberties Union, one of the most pressing privacy concerns associated with information systems is electronic surveillance, which involves software monitoring and recording a person's activities on the Internet, such as the Web sites he visits.

Software Licensing

By using a software license, the publisher or designer of software can restrict the consumer's usage of it. These restrictions normally include the following:

- Limiting the number of copies the user can create for his or her own purposes.
- Imposing limitations on the user's ability to resell copies of the software.
- Imposing limitations on the user's ability to modify the software.

In most cases, before using the software, users must agree to the terms of the software license; only then can they access the full range of the application's abilities. There are two primary categories of software licenses: open source and proprietary. They have drastically different definitions on what constitutes ownership.

Open Source and Proprietary Software Licenses

Both open source and proprietary software licenses grant ownership of the software to the designer or publisher; therefore, users cannot claim they designed or created the software. Both types of licenses may also restrict the user's ability to document and alter the software; the types of restrictions they impose, however, vary considerably. For instance, proprietary licenses only grant the consumer a license to use the software. The publisher or designer retains full legal ownership, and consumers may have little or no right to alter and redistribute the software. Open source allows end-users to own a copy of the software, and places very few and sometimes no restrictions on their ability to copy, alter, and redistribute the software.

Intellectual Property and Accuracy Concerns

Historically, copyright laws have protected intellectual property. However, the Internet has created a number of copyright problems for software, music, various written documents and other types of intellectual property. At one time, a person could only acquire these items by purchasing them; however, the Internet has made many of them available at no cost.

Information technology, specifically the Internet, allows tremendous quantities of information to be disseminated to the general public. Unfortunately, no one ensures the accuracy of this information. This is problematic because people generally believe what they read and see on Web sites—just as they believe print publications and television news broadcasts.

Workplace Impact of Information Technology

Information systems technology has profoundly altered how people work at their jobs. It has led to the creation of virtual teams, telecommuting, and other means of long-distance electronic communication. In modern times, workers throughout many different industries are performing their entire job functions at computer workstations. This has caused a number of physical and psychological health issues. For instance, because people who work on computers perform repetitive tasks, they are more likely to develop repetitive strain injuries, such as carpal tunnel syndrome. From a psychological standpoint, constant computer interaction causes many people to feel dehumanized. These health issues have led to a renewed focus on job design and ergonomics, or human factors, which attempts to increase the comfort and usability of workplace components, such as chairs and desks. With commerce becoming more automated and computerized, many customers also feel dehumanized.

Ergonomics and Job Design

The goal of ergonomics (or the science of human factors) is designing a job environment that increases the health and productivity of its workers. With the proliferation of information technology and the computer's emergence as the primary medium for performing work, the number of repetitive strain injuries has increased and workers are feeling more dehumanized by their jobs. Therefore, in ergonomics, designers seek to create workplace equipment (chairs, tables, keyboard, etc.) that prevents such injuries and increases worker well-being.

The goals of job design are humanizing the work environment, increasing job satisfaction, decreasing employee problems such as grievances and unsafe working conditions, and improving work efficiency and productivity. Job design specifically examines social factors, such as the awards and recognition available for doing a good job.

Telecommuting

Telecommuting (also known as working from home, working at home, and e-commuting) is one benefit of information technology. It enables workers to perform their job duties from a location other than the workplace. In most cases, this location is their home; however, due to the development and proliferation of new mobile communications technologies, employees can work from a wide variety of locations, such as parks, coffee houses, restaurants, etc. There are several potential advantages to telecommuting:

- Reduces the environmental impact and air pollution cause by car travel and commuting.
- Reduces traffic congestion.
- Offers employment opportunities to a wider range of people, such as stay-at-home parents and the disabled.
- Expands the pool of available workers that businesses can hire.
- Saves money for both individual workers and their employers.
- Improves the well-being and work/life balance of employees.

Telecommuting requires a result-based management style rather than an observation-based management style.

Virtual Team

A virtual team, or geographically dispersed team, uses information technology to collaborate and perform job functions across long distances and between different organizations and departments. The development and implementation of new fiber optic technologies have made virtual teams an integral component of most organizations, and have expanded the talent pool from which businesses hire. No longer is geography a restriction in the hiring processes; businesses can simply hire the best available person, regardless of location. He or she can communicate with the team electronically without ever meeting them in person. One popular application of virtual teams is offshore ISD. Organizations contract out software development or R&D work to a third-party offshore service provider, and interact with them electronically.

Knowledge Management

Knowledge management, or KM, is an attempt to generate, identify, and share insights and experiences that can expand the knowledge base of an organization. The goal of KM is improving organizational processes and performance, encouraging innovation, facilitating continuous improvement and integration, and providing lessons learned. It also helps the avoidance of redundant work, adaptation to new environments, and employee training. KM includes a number of strategies and practices intended to elicit insights and experiences.

These strategies include the following:

- Having people share their experiences through reporting.
- Asking experts to share their knowledge.
- Offering rewards to those who share some insight or experience.
- Transferring knowledge within the organization by means of storytelling.
- Offering apprenticeships.
- Learning through social software.
- Maintaining knowledge repositories, such as databases.
- Using collaborative technologies, such as groupware.

Globalization, Outsourcing, and Insourcing

Globalization occurs when communication and trade cause the economic and cultural integration of different societies. With its ability to provide instantaneous communication between multiple points across the globe, information technology has been one of the primary drivers of globalization.

Outsourcing describes the practice of subcontracting labor to an independent party—i.e., one outside the organization or business. In popular usage, outsourcing often implies the acquisition of labor from other countries. This is a common practice of multinational corporations, who cross national boundaries to subcontract labor. Because information technology allows organizations to acquire employees from anywhere, regardless of geographical location, it has enhanced outsourcing.

Insourcing describes the practice of using internal resources to perform work. In this way, it takes the opposite approach of outsourcing. Insourcing can imply that a business is using internal specialists, or that it is hiring labor from within its own country. Organizations may choose to insource to protect company secrets or to save money.

Business Strategies

Competition occurs when multiple businesses and individuals compete to gain a larger share of the market. In theory, competition creates an economic environment that encourages innovation in product, service, and technological development; increases the selection and quality of products available to consumers; and keeps prices lower than other economic models. Competition is one reason for proliferation and diversity in information technology.

Reengineering involves analyzing the processes and workflows within organizations. Processes are simply sequences of logically order tasks that should complete a certain function. In many cases, the goal of reengineering is consolidating several different processes into cross-functional processes, thereby increasing the efficiency and productivity of business operations.

Reengineering has helped create knowledge management, enterprise resource planning, groupware, collaborative systems, and many similar systems.

E-commerce, or electronic commerce, describes the use of information technology and networks to buy and sell products and services. One of the common networks systems for e-commerce is the

Internet. The vast majority of electronic transactions makes use of the World Wide Web and E-mail at some point.

Business process modeling, or BPM, is the method by which enterprise processes are modeled using various techniques and diagrams so they can be analyzed and improved. BPM may use information technology as part of modeling and analysis. Improved processes are implemented via change management.

TQM, or total quality management, describes a management technique whose goal is reducing product errors to one per one million units produced. In addition, TQM seeks to modernize equipment, increase worker competency, make supply chain management more efficient, and improve customer satisfaction.

Interpersonal and Group Processes and Characteristics

World Wide Web

The World Wide Web is one of the three most important services offered by the Internet. Although the terms World Wide Web and Internet are often used interchangeably, they are not the same. The Internet is a system that connects computer networks across the globe. Conversely, the World Wide Web (WWW) is a standard of the Internet, and consists of numerous interlinked hypertext documents. The information in these documents—text, images, videos, various types of multimedia—can be accessed through web pages. There are several concepts related to the WWW:

- Point and click access via hypertext links
- Uniform Resource Identifier
- Uniform Resource Locator
- HyperText Markup Language
- HyperText Transfer Protocol
- Web page
- Web site
- Web browser
- Search engine

Enterprise Resource Planning Software

ERP software has the following applications:

- Access control - restricts and manages user privileges within processes.
- Customer relationship management - includes sales, marketing, customer service, call support center, and commissions.
- Data services - are the manual interfaces used by customers, suppliers, and employees.
- Financials - includes fixed assets, accounts payable, accounts receivable, and managing cash flow.
- Human resources - includes payroll, benefits, time and attendance, training, and other aspects related to employees.
- Manufacturing - encompasses a wide range of activities related to manufacturing, such as quality control, cost management, engineering, engineering, processes, bill of materials, etc.

- Project management – includes managing activities, costing, billing, expenses, and performance.
- Supply chain management – includes inventory, purchasing, order entry, order to cash, figuring commissions, claims processing, supplier scheduling, and planning supply chains.

Customer Relations Management

Customer relations management, or CRM, is a type of ES that supports a company's efforts to manage its relationship with clients. The primary concerns of CRM are finding and attracting new clients, retaining current clients, retrieving former clients, and finding more cost effective means of marketing and handling clients. CRM focuses on sales activities, customer service, technical support, and marketing, and has the following benefits: it increases sales productivity and overall profitability; lowers expenses; facilitates communication; improves the organization's ability to profile and target potential clients; increases efficiency of sales and marketing processes; improves cross-selling and up-selling; improves customer service, call center efficiency, and customer retention; increases the company's market share; and leads to higher close rates.

Hardware and Systems Technology

Hardware, Software, and Operating System

Hardware applies to the monitor, tower, CPU, printer, scanner, various drives, and any other electronic component that comprises the computer.

Software differs from hardware. It applies to any program that controls computer functions and manages the output seen by the user. When a computer is first purchased, it will usually include software in the form of an operating system.

Operating system, or OS, manages and controls all computer functions, such as calculations and the processing of data. It is the master control system, determining the manner in which data is sent to the hardware devices that make up the computer. One of the most popular operating systems is Microsoft Windows.

Central Processing Unit

The central processing unit, or CPU, is the computer's primary microprocessor. It manages all computer functions, and implements the instructions within every software program. These instructions are stored in the computer's memory. Every CPU has an operating speed, which determines the speed at which the software will perform. Additionally, CPUs consist of three primary components—an arithmetic logic unit, a control unit, and a set of registers—and carry out the following functions:

- Fetch – retrieves the program instructions stored in the computer's memory.
- Decode – divides the instructions into portions that are usable by specific parts of the computer.
- Execute – connects different parts of the computer so the function can be performed.
- Writeback – commits the outcome of the execute step to computer memory.

Intel and AMD manufacture the majority of microprocessors that run in personal computers. Common PC microprocessors include Intel's Pentium, Celeron, and i-Series lines, and AMD's Phenom, Athlon and Sempron lines.

CPU Components

An arithmetic logic unit, or ALU, carries out the standard arithmetic functions of the CPU, such as addition and subtraction, as well as the standard logical functions of the CPU, such as AND, OR, NOT, and other operators.

A control unit manages the operations and functions performed by software instructions. It essentially functions as the computer's brain, and the CPU would be unable to function without it.

A processor register, also known as a general purpose register, is a small storage space that contains values relevant to implementing certain instructions. It is contained within a set of registers in the CPU. Although not included in the computer's memory capacity, process registers allow the CPU to access information more quickly than any other memory component; this is helpful for frequently used values.

Instruction Set

The instruction set contains keywords that identify each of the various operations stored performed by the CPU. This set contains the following keywords:

- Arithmetic instructions: add, subtract, and other math functions.
- Data instructions: move, store, load, input, output, etc.
- Control flow instructions: return, call, if, goto, etc.
- Logic instructions: add, subtract, not, etc.

Reduced instruction set computer, or RISC, is a type of CPU that supports only those instructions that run specialized applications. The goal of RISC is enhancing performance by simplifying instructions and, thereby, decreasing the execution time.

Complex instruction set computer, or CISC, is type of CPU that increases processing speed by executing around 100 instructions at one time. This is done by performing several low-level operations (such as arithmetic functions, load from memory, and memory store) in one instruction.

Computer Memory

Hard disk, also known as a disk drive or hard drive, is a computer hardware device that stores information electronically upon platters in a sealed enclosure.

Random-access memory, or RAM, is a temporary set of storage which allows applications to table relevant information for quick retrieval. Because RAM is many times faster in its data transfer times than a hard disk, applications such as video games or word processors, for instance, which have massive amounts of data which must be retrieved quickly and will be re-used often (in this case, large textures or the text being edited, respectively) will use RAM instead of having to re-read from the hard disk over and over. The computer can both read and write information into RAM memory.

Random-access means stored data can be accessed in any order, independent of physical location, unlike magnetic and optical disks.

Read-only memory, or ROM, is storage to which the computer is only capable of reading. Compact disks (CDs) are an example of Read-only memory, in that a commercial application's disk cannot be modified, but only read. It is this reason why CDs are often dubbed "CD-ROM".

Portable Data Storage Devices

Portable data storage devices include floppy disks, diskettes, compact discs, flash drives, and any other information storage media that is easily movable. These provide a more mobile alternative to a hard disk, which can normally only be moved with the entire computer. Much like a hard disk, data storage devices store information in files. Each file is a reference to a particular segment of data on the storage media, which might link to a word processing document, image, music file, or any other media. These files allow users to view the data on a disk in a useful and organized manner. Floppy disks are largely obsolete and have been replaced by CD-R/CD-RW, DVD-R/DVD-RW and Flash media. Flash drives are smaller and more durable than most other portable data storage devices, and have greater storage capacity. Also, Flash media can be written to an almost unlimited number of times, while CD-RW and DVD-RW will degrade with each overwrite, and CD-R and DVD-R can only be written once. Furthermore, a CD can only store around 700 megabytes of data, while a DVD can store 4-7 gigabytes, and flash media has no real theoretical limit, with common sizes ranging from 8-64 gigabytes (11-91 times the storage size of a CD!). Flash drives connect through a USB port on a computer.

Computer Devices

An Input device is any device used to enter information into a computer. Examples include keyboards, mouse, microphones, webcams, and light pens.

An Output device is any device that finds and presents processed information stored within the computer's memory. Examples include monitors, printers and speakers.

A Peripheral device is any electronic device that is external to the computer and attached to it in someway, such as through a wire or radio connection. Peripheral devices are not part of the system architecture, and can provide either input or output functions. Examples include scanners, printers, mouse, keyboards, touch screens, tape drives, microphones, webcams and cameras.

A keyboard is an input device that enables the user to communicate with the CPU and software. Keyboards contain various symbols—letters, numbers, and punctuation—and control commands that the user enters simply by pressing the appropriate button, which sends a unique electrical signal to the CPU.

A monitor is an output device that displays various messages to the user. Applications which have visual representations (such as most programs which do not simply run in the background) will instruct the graphics processor to prepare information for output to the monitor.

A mouse is an input device the user operates by moving around over a flat service and clicking buttons. Movement of the mouse corresponds to movement of a cursor displayed on the monitor. By moving the cursor over a specific data file and clicking the buttons on the mouse, the user can access the file.

A scanner is an input device that can copy and record paper documents, photographs, and other types of pictures into the computer's memory.

A touch screen is an input device that uses a pressure-sensitive panel. The user enters information by pressing a specific area on the panel.

A bar code reader is an input device common in business. It reads the bar code of a particular product, and identifies it to the computer. Warehouse applications make substantial use of bar code readers.

A point-of-sale, or POS, terminal is an input device that serves as a computerized cash register. It inputs items sold, item price, payment method, and other information related to merchandising.

A digital camera takes and records pictures. As an input device, it can connect to a computer (usually through a USB port) and download pictures onto the hard drive.

A printer is an output device capable of creating paper copies of documents, including text files, pictures, and graphs. Certain printers are designed solely to perform specialty functions, such as printing pictures.

PC speakers are output devices that allow computers to produce sound. They are especially important for certain kinds of software systems (such as music programs) and web sites that have sound or music accompaniment. Sound also allows the computer to alert the user.

Personal Computers

A personal computer, or PC, is any computer designed for use by a single individual without intervening operators. It has a separate operating system, and is considerably smaller and less expensive than mainframe computers and large data processing systems; consequently, it possesses reduced processing capability and speed. Desktop computers, laptops, tablet PCs, and handheld PCs are examples of personal computers, most of which offer the following software applications: word processing, database, spreadsheet, Email, web browsing, gaming, and other types of personal productivity and specialty software. Most PCs use an Intel x86 or x64-compatible microprocessor with a Windows Operating System—this is known as the Wintel platform. PCs are suitable for both home and the workplace, and are capable of running high speed internet and being connected through a LAN.

Personal Digital Assistants

A personal digital assistant, or PDA, is a mobile, handheld computer that manages personal information (appointments, addresses, memos) and provides wireless networking features, such Internet access. It has an electronic visual display that can show web pages and other documents. Newer versions possess audio speakers and touch screens, and can function as mobile phones or portable media players. PDAs typically possess the following features:

- Touch screen – The user can interact with the touch screen using a detachable stylus, usually through a virtual keyboard or by writing letters on the screen.
- Memory card – PDAs have slots and ports that support flash drives and SB cards.
- Wired connectivity – PDAs can connect to a computer though USB cable.
- Wireless connectivity – Bluetooth and Wi-Fi connectivity are common features on most PDAs.
- Synchronization – PDAs can receive immediate updates from a PC.

Mainframe Computers

Mainframe computers can carry out millions of instructions per second, and are operated by multiple users. Developed mostly in the 1960s, mainframe computers are mainstays in large companies, who require a system capable of processing large amounts of data and carrying out important applications, such as enterprise resource planning, financial transaction planning, and industry and consumer statistics. In addition to their lightning-quick computation speeds, they are known for their use of redundant systems, high reliability, tight security, backward compatibility (i.e. they can work with output generated by older software), and high utilization rate that enables them to handle large amounts of throughput. A mainframe can host multiple operating systems, which allows it to function like several virtual machines working in conjunction rather than a single computer.

Client/Server Architecture

Client/server architecture distributes tasks and workloads between servers (or service providers) and service requesters (or clients). The client/server system relies on distributed application architecture, in which multiple independent computers exchange information over a computer network, usually for purposes of solving a problem or fulfilling a goal. In a client/server system (such as the Internet), client computers exchange information with server machines, which operate as network hosts by running various server software programs. Client computers do not actually divulge any of their information. They only send requests to the server machines, which provide resources and services. Advantages of client/server architecture include the following:

- Redundancy - Because multiple independent computers carry out all tasks and functions, users seldom notice when one server must be replaced or repaired.
- Accommodation - The network can be used by a variety of clients and for a variety of uses.

Mainframe Vs Client/Server Architectures

Traditionally, mainframe architectures have relied on a single, centralized computer to carry out all tasks and functions. Conversely, client/server architectures rely on multiple, autonomous computers working together to run all applications—this type of system is known as a network. A prime example of client/server architecture and network computing is the Internet, whose main application protocols—HTTP, SMTP, Telnet, and DNS—operate using the client/server model. Internet clients are the web browsers, Email client, and online chat clients. They send request to the Internet servers, who are the web servers, mail servers, database servers, name servers, file servers, etc. Today, as businesses seek to decentralize their computing systems, even mainframe computers are turning away from their traditional centralized architecture and moving towards the client/server model.

Binary and ASCII

Binary Digits, Bit, Byte, and Binary-Coded Decimal

A binary digit can be either a 1 or a 0. It is the most basic unit of electronic information storage. Because computers can read only two digits, their arithmetic is base 2 (as opposed to base 10, which is standard human arithmetic). In binary language, the numbers 0 and 1 are represented as 0 and 1 respectively. However, the numbers 2, 3, and 4 are represented in binary as 10, 11, and 100 respectively. When performing numeric calculations, the internal computer works in binary. The operating system then converts the output of those calculations into the base 10 (decimal) system with which humans are familiar, and sends them through an output device.

A bit is a single binary digit.

A byte is a measurement of computer memory. It consists of eight bits in a row, and thus has a maximum decimal size of 256 values (2^8).

Binary-Coded Decimal, Extended Binary Coded Decimal Interchange Code, and American Standard Code For Information Interchange

Binary-coded decimal, or BCD, is a system for storing large numbers in which every decimal digit is stored as a 4-bit binary number.

Extended binary coded decimal interchange code, or EBCDIC, is the method by which IBM mainframe computers store letters and text.

American standard code for information interchange, or ASCII, is the method by which personal computers store letters and text. In both the EBCDIC and ASCII, the computer stores each language symbol—including letters of the alphabet, punctuation marks, dollar signs, etc.—as a single byte.

Both methods can hold a maximum of 256 characters, and neither is well-suited for symbol-heavy languages, such as Chinese. The only difference between the methods is the ASCII only uses seven of the eight bits that comprise the byte.

Picture File Formats

Joint photographic experts group, or JPEG, is a format for storing pictures within a computer. A JPEG consists of a grid of pixels, which can display up to 16.7 million different color variations.

Pixels are the smallest parts of an image that a screen, printer, or other output device can generate.

Tagged image file format, or TIFF, is a format for storing scanned photographs.

Graphics interchange format, or GIF, is capable of compressing graph and graphics files for electronic storage.

Moving picture experts group, or MPEG, is capable of compressing digital videos and animation for electronic storage.

Telecommunications

Telecommunication describes the sending of computer information over any network. Originally, the term only applied to the sending of computer information through the public telephone network.

Networks

A network is any computer system that links multiple computers. The link can be established physically or wirelessly. A network provides an effective means of sharing information and resources, such as data files, printer access, and software applications. Computers on the network can communicate with each other and use the same master software program. When a computer connects to the network, it becomes a network node and ceases to be considered a personal computer because its resources are shared. All networks have the following characteristics:

- Two or more linked computers.
- Network operating system that manages the sharing of peripheral devices.
- Unique network address for each network node.

Network Interface Card, Cable, Wireless Network Adapter, Network Node, Online, and Offline

A network interface card enables a computer to connect to a network. Each computer on the network must have an interface card.

Cables provide a physical means for connecting computers to a network.

Wireless network adaptors enable the creation of a wireless network. They allow computers to be linked through antennas rather than physical connections, such as cables.

A network node is any computer linked to the network. Linked computers lose their status as personal computers because they share resources.

Online is a term applied to computers that are active on the network. Offline is a term applied to computers that are not active on the network. This is usually because the user has decided to bring his computer offline or a malfunction has occurred.

Local Area Network

A local area network, or LAN, is a type of network in which all nodes reside in the same close physical space, such as a home, office, school, airport, or group of buildings clustered together.

LANs can be connected either physically using cables or wirelessly using network adaptors and antennas. The most common connection technologies are Ethernet over twisted-pair cabling and Wi-Fi. Other technologies include ARCNET and Token Ring. If a LAN is connected through cables, it will have a network hub—a centralized hardware device through which all wiring runs and to which are nodes are connected. Because LANs cover small geographic areas, they usually offer faster data transfer rates than other types of network and do not require their users to lease telecommunication lines. There are two primary types of LAN architecture: peer-to-peer, and client/server.

Peer-To-Peer Architecture

Peer-to-peer, also known as P2P, is a type of distributed network architecture in which all nodes make certain data files and resources—processing power, disk storage, network bandwidth, etc.—available to every other node. Unlike client/server architecture, P2P is an egalitarian network system; there are no dedicated servers that only provide resources and dedicated clients that only use resources. Every node on P2P functions as both a client and server, sharing information and in turn providing it. There are a number of advantages to P2P: It is ideal for file sharing. And, as more nodes are added to the network, more resources come available and system capacity increases. Conversely, in a client/server network, system resources only diminish as more nodes are added. Examples of P2P networks include Usenet, Napster, Gnutella, and Freenet.

Server and File Server

A server runs programs and contains both files and larger database files. In a client/server network, a server is a centralized, dedicated computer to which client computers connect and pull information. Most client/server networks have multiple servers, and each one fulfills a specific function. In P2P architecture, all nodes are servers.

A file server is responsible for running application programs and storing information that is used specifically by workstation nodes. Additionally, file servers are responsible for locking information when too many network nodes are trying to access or update it at the same time. Client/server networks have dedicated file servers while every node on a P2P can function as a file server.

Print Server and Database Server

A print server is a network node responsible for regulating output files as they are sent to printers.

A single network computer can function as both a file server and a print server; however, in a client/server network with many nodes, there should be a dedicated print server to prevent backlogs. Print servers are most prevalent in companies that produce numerous documents and reports.

A database server stores the extensive database files that are required to run business applications. Although some file servers contain database information, they may require help from a dedicated database server to run larger business applications in an efficient manner. Client/server networks with many nodes will usually have dedicated database servers. In P2P architecture, every computer contains database files.

Web Server and Mail Server

A web server is a network node responsible for maintaining content on the World Wide Web (such as a web site), and is most prevalent in companies that do substantial business over the Internet. Most web servers perform the following functions:

- Virtual hosting – maintains multiple web sites using only one address.
- Large file supporting – can handle files larger than 2 GB using a 32 bit Operating System (32-bit operating systems used to have a 2 GB limit on file sizes).
- Bandwidth throttling – prevent network saturation by limiting response speed and, thereby, serving more clients.
- Server-side scripting – prevents Web server and Web site implementation from overlapping.

A mail server is a network node responsible for transferring Email messages from one computer to another computer. For the network to operate properly, both the mail server and workstations must be using compatible Email software. In most cases, transmissions are sent using the simple mail transfer protocol, or SMTP.

Hardware Vs Software In A Client/Server Database

In a client/server network, the term server has different meanings depending on whether it is used in relation to hardware or software applications. As a description of hardware, server applies to the computers that function as file, print, database, web, and mail servers. As a description of software, server applies to any computer that runs the main application programs or contains a database. The term client is somewhat different. In most cases, it describes only software—specifically, those programs run by workstation nodes, which are known as client workstations or client computers. This is an important distinction when taking the CLEP examination. Test takers should read questions very carefully to determine if the they are referring to the software or hardware aspects of a client/server database.

Network Topology and Star Network

Network topology is the manner in which nodes are arranged in a network, and can be either centralized or decentralized. There are three basic arrangements: star network, bus network, and ring network.

A star network is a centralized topography in which a central computer (also known as a switch or hub) connects all nodes and regulates network access. Star networks offer advantages:

- Greater security and more efficient management due to centralization.
- Increased speed and performance. Data packets pass through a maximum of three devices and two links rather than multiple nodes.
- Node isolation. If one node malfunctions, it has no effect on the other nodes.
- Simple arrangement. Complex routing and protocols are not necessary. Installing, removing, and repairing network components are relatively easy processes.

The major disadvantages are installation expense—each node requires a separate cable to connect to the hub—and total reliance on the central hub.

BUS NETWORK

A bus network is a type of network topography in which each node is linked sequentially. Bus networks have the following advantages:

- Installation is both simple and inexpensive because only one cable is used to link all nodes.
- Fewer wires create a lighter network.
- Creating and adding on to the network is relatively easy.
- Bus networks are best-suited for small, temporary network that do not have high speed requirements.
- Users can more easily identify network malfunctions and cable faults.

Bus networks have the following disadvantages:

- A single cable has limited length and, as such, can only connect a limited a number of nodes.
- A malfunction in one node can bring down the entire network.
- Adding additional stations reduces performance and speed.
- When two users transmit simultaneously, a collision may occur in the network. This necessitates the use of a collision-handling scheme, such as carrier sense multiple access.

Disconnecting one computer from the network is difficult because every computer is connected.

RING NETWORK

A ring network is a type of decentralized network topography in which each node links to two other nodes and the final node connects to the first node, making a ring configuration. As long as the network incorporates two-way communication, a node failure or cable break will not bring down the entire system. A ring network has the following advantages:

- It can manage connectivity without the aid of a network server.
- Transmission is carried out in a very orderly, structured manner with each node having access to the ring.
- It offers better performance than a star topology when the network load is heavy.

There are also certain disadvantages:

- Faulty ports and work stations can hinder network performance.
- Moving or adding components to the network can be problematic.
- Ring networks are slower than Ethernet connections when the network load is normal.
- Expense is often greater.

NETWORK OPERATING SYSTEM

A network operating system, or NOS, manages all activity on the network. A NOS is necessary because the operating systems for personal computers, such as Windows, are not designed to handle an entire network of computers. A NOS is capable of performing all administrative functions, such as tracking users and their connections, enforcing security protocols, implementing server back-up systems, and managing peripheral devices that are shared by multiple users.

Additionally, a NOS manages communication between the various nodes, also known as workstations, on the network. Some network operations systems are designed specifically for client/server networks, such as Windows Server, Novell Network, and Linux. Another example is Windows NT.

Network Protocol and Network Address

A network protocol regulates access to public data on the network. It locks a data file when two or more users are attempting to update it at the same time. This ensures that the no data is lost and no revisions are overwritten when the last copy of the file is saved. The ability to lock out data is especially important in the software industry where programs are written by a team. If multiple team members were allowed to access the program simultaneously, one programmer could potentially overwrite the updates of another programmer. A network address is a unique identifier assigned to each node on the network. Using this identifier, the network is able to distinguish between computers.

CSMA/CD

Carrier sense multiple access with collision detection, or CSMA/CD, is a method of managing and regulating access to information and resources available on a network. It is most effective for networks that are medium-sized and smaller. Using carrier sensing, CSMA/CD is capable of detecting collisions, which occur when two nodes are trying to access the same data at the same time. When a collision is detected, the CSMA/CD transmits a jam signal that stops both nodes from sending. Then, in order to determine which node is allowed first access to data, the network operating system generates a random number. This number represents the length of a time a node must wait before resending its request. CSMA/CD ensures that all computers have equal and fair access to network resources.

Token Passing

Token passing is a method of managing and regulating access to information on a network. It is most effective for larger networks, and relies on an electronic signal known as a token, which is passed around between nodes. A node is only authorized to communicate across a network if it possesses the token. In order to determine which node gets the token, the network operating system uses round-robin scheduling, which provides each workstation with equal access to use network resources. Unlike a contention-based method such as CSMA/CD, token passing completely eliminates collisions—this allows more efficient use of bandwidth when network traffic is heavy. However, when network traffic is light, token passing is less efficient because each node must wait to receive a token.

Wide Area Network

A wide area network, or WAN, connects computers that do not reside in close physical proximity. It covers a much larger geographical area than a LAN, but uses same communication protocols as a LAN. There a number of options for establishing WAN connectivity:

- Leased line – links two computers or two WANs using a point-to-point connection. Although this method is the most secure, it is also the most expensive.
- Circuit switching – connects two endpoints using a dedicated circuit path. This method is the least expensive, but setting up the call service is often difficult.
- Packet switching – uses a carrier internetwork to transmit variable length packets through a point-to-point or point-to-multipoint link
- Cell relay – transmits fixed length packets over virtual circuits.

WANs communicate using simplex (meaning one direction), half-duplex (meaning one direction at one time), and full duplex (meaning both directions simultaneously using separate circuits).

Network Cabling

Network cabling is the process by which cables physically attach the different nodes of a network. In client/server architecture, cables connect the client workstations to the network servers. In peer-to-peer architecture, cables connect the client workstations to each other. With the development of wireless technology, cabling is gradually becoming obsolete; however, it is still in use in many networks, such as in-office and in-building. Network cabling can be divided into three standards: ARCnet, Ethernet, and token ring. Nodes are not interchangeable between standards. A node must be made compatible with a network's standard in order to function properly; only then can it translate the signals from workstations, servers, and peripheral devices.

ARCnet

ARCnet is an older network cabling standard for LAN protocols. It is almost totally obsolete and replaced by Ethernet systems. Designed for the first mainframe and IBM personal computers, ARCnet was compatible with a star topology, twisted pair cable, or coaxial cable. It relied on network interface cards and a token passing scheme to manage network access. The token passing scheme in ARCnet is deterministic, which means that a network station will always receive the token in a set amount of time. Consequently, ARCnet is ideal for embedded systems, process control markets, and other real-time networking systems, which impose operational deadlines on system response. In the past, ARCnet was less expensive and performed better under heavy loads than Ethernet, which is a collision-based system; however, as processor speeds began reducing the chance of collision and expense, and Ethernet proved to be many times faster, Ethernet systems became more popular.

Token Ring Network

A token ring network is a network cabling standard for LAN protocols. Developed by IBM, it is a non-collision based system that uses a 3-byte frame known as a token to regulate network access. Nodes can only transmit data if they possess the token, which is passed around to each workstation at a set interval. Upon reaching a workstation that needs to send information, the token is converted into a data frame for transmission. This method of regulating network access is known as token passing. A token ring combines both ring and star topologies. The network nodes are physically connected in the shape of a star; however, they are organized in a ring topology—information moves from one node to the next in sequential order. Token rings use twisted pair cable and originally supported 255 workstations.

Ethernet Cabling

Ethernet cabling is the most popular cabling standard in use by businesses today. Created by the Xerox corporation, an Ethernet network utilizes a bus topology that can support 1,024 workstations. It relies on a CSMA/CD (collision detection) system in order to regulate network access. Advances in processor technology have made collision detections systems more efficient and cheaper, thereby increasing the popularity of Ethernet systems. In most cases, nodes are linked physically through insulated four-pair twisted pair cables made of copper, which can accommodate both full-duplex and half-duplex communication protocols. Networks can achieve higher speeds by using different types of wiring, which range from 10BASE-T (slower) to 1000BASE-T (faster). Because these types of wiring use the same connectors, faster speeds can normally support lower speeds, allowing the network can combine different generations of equipment. The fastest Ethernets use fiber-optic cable.

Fiber-optic cable enables faster communication than copper-based wiring. It consists of thin fibers of glass that transmit laser light to optical detectors, which then convert the light into digital signals. Fiber-optic cable is designed for sophisticated, high speed networks. Its use is limited due to expense and the difficulty of installation and maintenance.

Modem

Modem, or modulator/demodulator, is a peripheral device. There are two primary varieties of modems: telephony and cable (television). While telephony modems (those that transmit signals over a telephone line) began as dial-up modems (originating as external components, moving into PCs as peripheral cards, and then moving externally once again with the advent of DSL), cable modems have always generally existed as external components. All modems convert digital information into analog signals, which are sound-based in telephony modems, and radio-frequency based in cable modems, and then transmit them at fixed speeds. The receiving computer transforms the analog signal back into digital information.

Communications Protocols

Asynchronous and Synchronous

Communication protocols allow computers to transmit information to other computers through a network or over telecommunications devices. These protocols ensure that both the sending and receiving computer interprets and handles signals in the same way. There are seven communication protocols: asynchronous, synchronous, full-duplex, half-duplex, double-duplex, echoplex, and parallel.

An asynchronous protocol sends information in sequential bits. A start bit marks the beginning of data transmission and stop bit marks the end. The transmission is not synchronized by a clock.

A synchronous protocol is intended for high speed data transfer. The transmission is synchronized according to electronic clock signals. Mainframe network computers use synchronous protocols due to their fast processing speeds.

Full-Duplex, Half-Duplex, Double-Duplex, Echoplex, and Parallel

Full-duplex is a type of asynchronous transmission. It enables the simultaneous sending and receiving of signals over the same communication channel.

Half-duplex, also known as a local echo, is a type of asynchronous transmission. It can send only one signal at a time over the same communication channel. Consequently, two computers must take turns when communicating between each other.

Double-duplex is a modified full-duplex transmission. Both ends of the communication channel have a sender and a receiver that transmit in both directions at the same time.

Echoplex is a communication protocol in which a computer signals that it has received a message by sending (or echoing) the message back to the computer that originally transmitted it.

Parallel is a type of synchronous transmission. A peripheral device, most often a printer, uses a parallel port to signal its readiness to receive information.

Operating System

An operating system manages the computer's primary hardware devices. As the base software, it performs a computer's primary functions:

- System supervision, which includes memory management, program control, and process control.
- Security, which involves regulating access to the system and files.
- Hardware services, which manage the keyboard, monitor, hard drive, and other hardware devices.
- Software services, which support file systems and user interfaces.
- Communication services, which manages communication between the computer and external systems or the local network.

Fax Machine

A fax machine uses the telephone line to send and receive digital copies of printed messages. Networks can incorporate fax machines as peripheral devices or use fax modems.

Memory Manager

A memory manager determines and allocates the amount of RAM necessary to run a program. In an operating system, memory managers can function in one of two possible ways:

- Monoprogramming – RAM can contain and execute only one program at once.
- Multiprogramming – RAM can contain and execute more than one program at once.

Although multiprogramming can involve running multiple programs simultaneously, it can also involve running the programs concurrently. In concurrent operation, the operating system holds multiple programs in RAM but only executes one at any given time. After a certain duration has passed, the operating system then moves to another program. Multiprogramming can be executed using a variety of techniques, including partitioning and paging.

Partitioning and Paging

Partitioning is a concurrent multiprogramming technique. The operating system sets aside an area in RAM known as a partition, which is capable of holding multiple programs. The system then executes each program one at time.

Paging refers to a type of virtual memory. The operating system separates the program into page segments, stores them on the hard disk, and then loads them into any open space in RAM. Paging requires less memory than partitioning because the program is not stored in memory its entirety; rather, it is broken down into segments that are scattered throughout the computer. In certain cases, paging can lead to thrashing, in which the operating system has difficulty transitioning between pages.

Process Manager, Spooler, and Interrupt Handler

A process manager controls programs (also known as processes) as they are executing in memory. A program will remain in memory until the user commands it to perform an input or output function, it completes its process, or it exhausts the time that the CPU has allowed it. A spooler is a software application that regulates access to the printer; rather than sending information directly to the printer, the spooler sends information into file storage to be printed at some time in the future. This prevents one program from dominating printer time. An interrupt handler is operating system software that examines and categorizes interrupt commands, which are signals that alert the CPU to stop a process so it can process a request, such as an I/O (input or output) or an error interrupt. For instance, upon receiving an I/O request, the interrupt handler will recognize its type and pass it on to the device manager.

Device Manager

A device manager, also known as an I/O supervisor, regulates access to I/O (input or output) devices. Regulation is necessary because I/O devices run at much slower speeds than the CPU; consequently, the CPU must wait until the device has completed its task before sending it another one. The device manager has three basic functions:

- Checking if the device is operating and capable of performing additional functions.
- Storing a queue or list of processes that require the device's attention.
- Assigning priority to the processes so that the device known which process to access first.

An I/O device includes a program known as a device driver that allows it to interact and function with the operating system.

Wireless Networks and Mobile Networks

A wireless network, sometimes known as a mobile network, consists of nodes and workstations that are linked through wireless technology, which communicates using electromagnetic waves. The advantages of a wireless network include portability and flexibility in network arrangement. The disadvantages include increased security risk, slower data flow rate and increased compatibility problems when connecting new nodes. There are several types of wireless networks:

- Wireless Personal Area Network (WPAN) – includes Wi-Fi networks, Fixed Wireless Data networks, and other small area networks. Bluetooth is a type of WPAN technology.
- Wireless Local Area Network (WLAN) – covers a local area, such as the inside of a home or a public business. Wi-Fi can be a type of LAN.
- Wireless Metropolitan Area Network (WMAN) – connects multiple WLANs.
- Wireless Wide Area Network (WWAN) – covers a wide outdoor area and usually serves to connect office buildings or provide public Internet access.
- Mobile devices networks.

Mobile Device Networks

Mobile device networks are a type of wireless network most often linked through cellular, or mobile phone, technology. Standards for mobile phone technology include GSM (Global System for Mobile Communication), PCS (Personal Communications Service), and D-AMPS (Digital-Advanced Mobile Phone Service).

A cellular, or mobile, phone supports a variety of functions related to wireless networking, such as voice communication, short message service (SMS) for text messaging, email, Internet access via packet switching, GPS, Bluetooth and multimedia messaging service (MMS) for transmitting photos and videos.

Bluetooth is a protocol that enables the wireless sending and receiving of information over short distances. Many devices contain a Bluetooth protocol, such as headsets, computers, video game consoles, etc.

Satellite modems and phones enable users to access the internet. Satellite Internet access is most prevalent in areas where conventional methods are unavailable.

Information Systems and Office Application Software in Organizations

Word Processing and Desktop Publishing Software

Word processing software is used to create text documents. It is capable of revising and printing documentation, and usually offers a number of editing features, such as a spelling and grammar checker, thesaurus, and formatting program. A user can often integrate graphics from other programs and perform mail-merge functions.

Desktop publishing software includes many features offered by standard word processing software but offers a greater variety of layout, formatting, and graphics options. Desktop publishing software is used to create a variety of documents and advertising copy, such as outdoor signs, announcements, newsletters, retail package designs, promotional displays, point of sale signs, trade show exhibits and other types of documentation. When using the program, users work in a WYSIWYG (What You See Is What You Get) page layout that presents an accurate digital image of the finished product.

Spreadsheet and Graphics Software

Spreadsheet software is used to generate spreadsheets in either traditional or newer formats. Spreadsheets consist of cells (or grid entries) into which users enter information. These cells are arranged into columns and rows that form a grid pattern. Most types of spreadsheet software offer what-if processing: If a user alters an entry in one of the cells, the remaining cells will automatically change to reflect the new value. A user can display a spreadsheet graphically or format it into a report.

Graphics software allows users to create visual displays, including maps, drawings, and graphs. Presentation graphics software offers a range options designed specifically for presentations, such as multiple font types, drawing tools, spell checker, templates, and clip art.

Speech Recognition, End-User Database, and Presentation Software

Speech recognition software understands and takes commands from human voice messages. Most programs can recognize between 30,000 and 75,000 words. There are two primary types of speech recognition software: discrete recognition, which is capable of understanding only one word at a time, and continuous recognition, which is capable of understanding multiple words spoken at a normal pace.

End-User databases are collections of data files created by users. These collections often include spreadsheets, download files, and documents created with word processing or desktop publishing software.

Presentation software packages help users create information displays. Most packages come with three basic features: editor for formatting and inserting text, the ability to insert graphics and a slideshow display system.

E-Mail, Voice Mail, and Fax

Electronic mail, or E-mail, describes any message that is digitally sent and received through a computer network or system of computer networks, such as the Internet. In order to retrieve a message, a user must access the network or system. One of the primary benefits of E-mail is that a single message can be sent to multiple users, such as a mailing list.

Voice mail is a digital recording of a voice message that is usually made via phone. Voice mail is particularly beneficial when the person being contacted is not immediately available.

Fax, or facsimile, is another method of transferring messages. The user writes his message onto a piece of paper, inserts it into his fax machine, and then dials the number of the receiving fax machine. Personal computers are also capable of sending faxes.

Electronic Meeting Systems

Electronic meeting systems (EMS) facilitate the process of group decision-making. They enable users to conduct meetings and hold conferences even when they are separated by significant geographical distances. In most cases, each meeting participant has his or her own computer or broadcast device. Participants can talk and interact as if they were speaking face-to-face; no one is required to wait for a turn or for the current speaker to yield the floor. Some electronic meeting systems allow for anonymous participation, which is valuable when the purpose of the meeting is generating and assessing ideas. A common electronic meeting system is teleconferencing, in which users interact over closed-circuit television broadcasting.

Work Group Computing

Work group computing enables multiple users to work cooperatively even if they are separated by long distances. It can describe any technology or system that contributes to the computer supported cooperative world, in which people interact for purposes of communication, coordination, cooperation, competition, and entertainment. Work group computing is most efficient when everyone in the group is using the same suite of applications. This ensures the applications will be compatible, data and procedures will be transferred easily between users, and the suite will achieve its maximum potential. Furthermore, bundled software applications tend to be cheaper. Work group computing is also referred to as computer-supported collaboration (CSC), collaborative work support systems (CWSS), and computer-based systems for collaborative work (CSCW).

Internet

The Internet is a vast global system that connects computer networks. In essence, it is a network of networks linked through numerous electronic and optical devices. Using the Internet Protocol Suite (TCP/IP), a user can connect with literally millions of people, businesses, organizations, and governments across the world. The Internet originated in the late 1960s through a US Department of Defense project known as ARPANET. After years of funding and research by various civilian organizations and the National Science Foundation, the technology was commercialized in the 1990s and came to form what is now known as the Internet. In 2009, at least one-quarter of the earth's population was connected to the Internet. In most cases, users are connected through an Internet Service Provider, or ISP, which charges a monthly fee. Certain ISPs are backbone networks, whose only purpose is connecting smaller service providers.

Internet Protocol Suite

The Internet Protocol Suite, or TCP/IP, consists of two different protocols: Internet protocol (IP) and the transmission control protocol (TCP). The TCP/IP provides a set of guidelines that regulate the flow of information over the Internet. When a message is sent between locations, it is first broken up into pieces of information known as packets, which include the following information:

- Sending address.
- Receiving address.
- Packet's correct sequence in the message.

Packets may take different paths through the Internet to reach their receiving addresses—even when they are all part of the same message. Once all packets that make up a message arrive at their target location, the receiving computer will use the TCP/IP to reassemble them in their correct order.

IP Addresses and Domain Names

An IP address is a unique identification number given to all computers that connect to the Internet. Every IP address has the same basic format: three dots separating four number sets, such as 123.45.678.910. Each set of numbers can range from 0 to 255.

A domain name is a unique identifier for commercial computers. Unlike an IP address, a domain name can use words, symbols, and numbers separated by dots. The first three symbols of a domain name are often www., (such as www.mo-media.com) specifying that it is a hypertext server, and not a different protocol such as ftp or news (nntp). The middle part of a domain name may incorporate any amount or combination of dots, letters, numbers, and symbols, with a few rules governing what is allowed, and how particular combinations (especially those using the period) function. The last part of the domain name (also known as the top-level domain) must include a suffix that identifies the type of site the user is visiting. The most common suffixes include the following:

- .com – indicates a commercial site.
- .edu – indicates an educational site.
- .gov – indicates a military site.
- .org – indicates the side of an organization or association.

Domain Names Must Use a Standardized Suffix.

Internet Services

The three most important services offered by the Internet include the following:

- Communication
- Information retrieval
- World Wide Web

Communication Services

Communication services include newsgroup, chatrooms, Internet telephone service, E-mail, and streaming audio and video. A popular E-mail protocol is the simple mail transfer protocol, or SMTP, which mail servers and mail transfer agents use to send and receive messages. User-level client mail applications use SMTP for sending mail, and other protocols—such as POP or IMAP—for receiving mail. Using a streaming audio and video (also known as a streaming media) communication service, users can view and listen to a message as it being transmitted. There is no waiting for the arrival and reassembly of the entire sequence of packets.

Information Retrieval Services

Information retrieval is one of the three most important services offered by the Internet. It uses the file transfer protocol (FTP) to connect to remote computers and retrieve data files from them. There are a number of software tools that facilitate data retrieval. Historically, one such tool is archie, which performed file searches on remote computers. Another tool is a gopher, which searches Internet servers for other linked gopher files and allows the user to move between sites in order to find certain information. Businesses use a special type of information retrieval software known as the Electronic Data Interchange. This enables the electronic exchange of invoices, purchases orders, and other pertinent business documents.

World Wide Web Terms

A Hyperlink allows the user to move between web pages on the World Wide Web. Web pages often include hyperlinks to other web pages that the user can access simply by clicking on the link.

A web page provides information that can be accessed through the World Wide Web. The information is normally formatted using HTML or XHTML.

A web site contains a number of web pages, images, videos, and other digital information media that are related and identified through a uniform resource locator, or URL. Before a user can display any information on the World Wide Web, he must have a web site on which to present said information, and the web site much have a home page, which will automatically load whenever the website is accessed.

A uniform resource identifier, or URI, identifies Internet resources—web pages, images, videos, and other digital information media—via a string of characters. Using World Wide Web protocols, a URI allows the user to view and interact with web pages. A URI has two subsets: a uniform resource locator and a uniform resource name.

A uniform resource locator, or URL, specifies the location of a particular Internet resource and the method for accessing the resource. The URL for a web site will include its domain name and, in some cases, a page identifier for a specific page within the site.

A uniform resource name, or URN, identifies the name of a particular Internet resource. It does not identify the location of the resource. A URL and URN have complimentary functions.

Hypertext markup language, or HTML, is the most common markup language for web pages. It allows users to structure and format documents on the World Wide Web. They can insert structural semantics, such as text, paragraphs, lists, menus, and online help information; embed images and objects; and create interactive forms.

Hypertext transfer protocol, or HTTP, is a transfer protocol that determines the formatting and transmission of information on the WWW. Using the HTTP protocol, users (clients) send requests to web sites (servers), who then send back a response. The interaction between client and web site may occur through a variety of intermediaries, such as gateways and tunnels. HTTP locates Web resources using their Uniform Resource Locators (URL).

A browser is a type of Web software. It allows users to retrieve, display, and navigate (usually via hyperlinks) information resources on the World Wide Web. Common information resources include web pages, videos, pictures, and other multimedia displays. These are identified by their URLs.

Surfing describes the act of looking through and accessing Web links in hopes of finding pertinent or useful information.

Spamming is a type of Internet abuse. It involves distributing junk E-mail to users who have not asked for the information.

Flaming is a type of Internet abuse. It involves sending obscene or offensive messages to other users. These messages are commonly found in E-mail exchanges, but are present in virtually every form of Internet exchange, such as chat rooms and threaded discussions.

A search engine is a software application that provides links to Web sites based on information given by the user. The user simply inputs a word or phrase into the application, and it generates a list of Web sites that include the word or phrase. In order to appear in the link list, a site must be registered with the search engine. Registration occurs when the search engine is alerted of the site's existence either by the site's creator or a web crawler.

A web crawler scans the Web automatically and identifies sites for the search engine to use at a later date.

A metasearch engine inputs the word or phrase provided by the user into multiple search engines.

Analytical Processing

Analytical processing software serves a variety of functions. It can structure data in either graphic or report formats, and offers a variety of decision-making tools, such as projections, comparisons, decision analysis, and statistical inferences. Additionally, many types of analytical processing software are capable of generating statistical and mathematical models of real world scenarios. These models, which can be displayed graphically, are derived from queries and information submitted via a user interface. Most managers can use analytical process software to support their decision-making process regardless of their specific function or responsibility within the company.

Two common types of analytical process software are decision support systems and executive information systems.

Decision Support Systems and Executive Information Systems

A decision support system, or DSS, is a common type of analytical processing software. It aids decision makers within businesses and organizations by gathering and analyzing various types of information, such as documents, personal data, and models. This information is then used to solve problems. An executive information system, or EIS, is a specialized form of DSS that supports senior level executives as they implement the organization's strategic goals. In most cases, a DSS or EIS consists of three basic parts:

- Data management application – includes a specialized database with data mining capability
- User interface – allows the user to input ad-hoc queries into the database, which often generates a graphical output.
- Model management application – offers "what-if" process. The user can analyze real-world possibilities by changing values within the model.

Geographic Information System

A geographic information system, or GIS, gathers, stores, analyzes, and displays information related to locations. It combines cartography, database technology, and decision support system (DSS) software, and can generate maps and other types of graphical representations of geographic locations. In business, organizations use GIS technology in order to locate sites for new businesses for underserved markets.

Global Positioning System

A global positioning system, or GPS, relies on GIS technology to determine the precise geographic location of its users. It can also provide information on timing and navigation for a variety of activities, including driving, flying, and sailing. In business, GPS technology is especially useful for tracking units anywhere in the world. It is also useful for map-making, surveying, surveillance, and commerce.

Group Decision Support Systems

A group decision support system, or GDSS, supports meetings and group work by enabling multiple users to exchange their thoughts and ideas, and to engage in complex decision-making. In most cases, users collaborate through a shared computer or network, or an electronic meeting system. Though similar on some levels, GDSS should not be confused with computer supported cooperative work (CSCW); GDSS is task-oriented while CSCW is focused on communication. GDSS technology can operate under four possible conditions: same time and same place; same time but different place; different time and different place; and, different time but same place. The advantages of GDSS include improvements in communication, synergy, objectivity, individual participation, and learning. The disadvantages include slow feedback, inefficient use of information, excessive amounts of information, and an increase in Internet abuses.

Knowledge-Based Information and Expert Systems

A knowledge-based information system is a type of DSS software that integrates a branch of computer science known as artificial intelligence (AI), in which computers are programmed to consider multiple hypotheses and extrapolate inferences. One type of knowledge-based information system is an expert system, which applies AI methods in order to solve problems or remove uncertainties in specific areas of expertise. Expert systems are used in situations where humans would normally be consulted, and are capable of the following tasks: offering advice in a specific knowledge area, performing problem-solving functions, providing answers to user questions and explaining the reasoning behind those answers.

Business Informatics

Business informatics, or BI, combines three separate fields into a single discipline: informatics, information technology, and management concepts. Informatics covers a wide range of topics, including the science of information, information processing, and the creation of information systems. Essentially, informatics seeks to understand how systems structure, acquire, access, process, and communicate information. Business information is specifically concerned with the interaction between the three systems that comprise most organizations:

- Activity system – a group of activities undertaken by people within organizations. These activities are designed to generate a specific action or fulfill a business process.
- Information system – communication between people within organizations. It supports an activity system by acquiring, processing, communicating, and using information that furthers business processes.
- Information and communication technology (ICT) system – is the technology (hardware, software, etc.) that facilitates communication between people within organizations. It supports an information system.

Enterprise Systems

An enterprise system, or ES, is a type of packaged application software. It integrates multiple software and information technology applications into a single system and, thereby, enhances their ability to perform computation, store data, and transmit data. In business organizations, an ES supports process completion, communication, reporting, and analysis of data. Although enterprise systems vary between businesses, they all share certain characteristics: they extend throughout the entire organization (enterprise-wide), achieve integration via centralized databases and middleware, work in real-time, package together multiple pieces of application software, and provide support by carrying out processes and coordinating work. Additional characteristics common to ES software include the following: it has a wide-ranging impact on the work of people within the organization, requires extensive training to operate, offers much flexibility and can be altered to fit new needs. Common types of ES include enterprise resource planning (ERP), customer relationship management (CRM), and supply chain management (SCM).

Enterprise Resource Planning

Enterprise resource planning, or ERP, is a type of ES that combines all business functions, and manages the flow of information between those functions and people within the organization and between the organization and its stakeholders. This information includes both external and internal resources, such as human resources, tangible assets, financial assets and materials. An ERP system integrates a number of different computer-based systems and software applications into a single, uniform enterprise system by using a centralized database and shared computing platform. An ERP system can be configured in one of two ways: a centralized server design, or a distributed design. In the latter configuration, the ERP is distributed across multiple modular hardware and software units that are connected through a Local Area Network (LAN). These units communicate with and provide services to their users. The distributed design offers greater flexibility: The business can simply combine modules from different vendors rather than copying entire computer systems.

Customer Relations Management

CRM has the following applications:

- Customer service and support – the tools that organizations use to assist clients with their problems, improve efficiency, and lower costs. Call support centers are one example.
- Interdepartmental – improves the relationship and communication between the various departments that comprise an organization (marketing, service, etc.). Technical support centers are one example.
- Marketing – measures the effectiveness of advertising campaigns in a variety of media—email, direct mail, social media, etc.
- Sales analytics – include predictive analytics, which assess the effectiveness of various advertising strategies, and key performance indicators, which help determine customer behaviors and preferences.
- Sales force automation – automates much of the mundane work of the sales process, such as data entry, so that the sales representative can spend more time pursuing clients
- Contact manager system – often used by small businesses to streamline customer interaction.

This system integrates email, faxes, scheduling, and other aspects of customer interaction.

Social media – sites such as Facebook and Twitter. CRM can help organizations use these sites to their advantage.

Supply Chain Management Software

Supply chain management software, or SCMS, is a type of ES that helps manage supply chain interactions, supplier relationships, and business processes. In most cases, SCMS is capable of processing customer requirements and purchases orders, and managing inventory, good receipts, the warehouse, suppliers, and sourcing. It may also enable electronic transactions with supply chain partners via integration technology. SCMS systems often incorporate forecasting tools. Using algorithms and consumption analysis, these tools find a balance between supply and demand, make business processes more efficient, and predict future needs. SCMS systems are generally not as comprehensive as enterprise resource planning (ERP) systems. In fact, users can often purchase a standalone SCMS system to address a specific need, such as improving inventory efficiency or supplier relationships.

Electronic Data Interchange

Electronic data interchange, or EDI, is the electronic transfer of information between organizations. The structure of this transfer must follow the X12 series guidelines, which were established by the US national standards body. EDI goes beyond the capabilities of more common digital sending and retrieval systems such as E-mail; EDI allows businesses to change and update invoices, purchases orders, checks, and other pertinent business documents. In addition to the X12 series guidelines, EDI messages must meet other criteria as well: They cannot include monetary instruments, and they can be transmitted though computer only—either through telecommunications or electronic storage media. Human interference should be necessary only if an error arises or a quality review is required. Most electronic commerce transactions around the world use the EDI format.

Proprietary Software

Proprietary describes a type of software. Proprietary software is developed for a particular company to be used only by that company. The company can either create the software in-house or contract it out to a software development firm. Proprietary implies that a program is not free or open source. Instead, it has a copyright owner who can restrict its usage. In most cases, users are forbidden from using the software's full range of abilities, modifying it for their own private purposes, or copying multiple versions of it. Proprietors can implement these restrictions using legal and/or technical methods. Legal methods often involve obtaining copyrights, licenses, or patents. Technical methods include distributing closed-source programs that only computers can read and that hide the source code with which humans can work.

Commercial Off-The-Shelf Software

Commercial off-the-shelf (also known as COTS or package) describes a type of software. COTS is designed specifically for use by the general public, who can acquire it from vendors. In most cases, vendors sell, license, or lease the software to consumers; however, it is sometimes free. Many businesses and government agencies use package software because it is cheaper to procure and maintain than proprietary software. COTS requires less time and fewer resources to develop than proprietary software, which must be designed starting from nothing. However, using COTS also poses a number of drawbacks—specifically, a lack of software integration among the company's systems, dependence on a vendor, and less control over future versions of the software.

Database Management System

A database management system, or DBMS, consists of a group of software applications that manage information within a database, including its creation, storage, organization, and retrieval. A DBMS ensures data integrity, and regulates who can access the database and who can develop and control the information contained therein. For the task of development and control, most organizations appoint database administrators. In order to access the database, an end user submits a request through the DBMS using query language, which must conform to one of the appropriate application protocols. This language specifies the database's organization, and the access and use of its information. There are several database models, including hierarchical, network, relational, distributed, object-oriented, and hypermedia.

Presentation Graphics Software

Presentation graphics software supports the creation of audience presentations. It normally includes an editing application for inserting and formatting text, an application for inserting and moving graphics, and a slide show application for displaying images that aid the speaker. This software can prepare a range of presentation-types, including professional, academic, and entertainment. It can present slides either in printed form (handouts, pamphlets, etc.) or, more commonly, on a display screen that the user can navigate. When the slides are presented electronically, they can feature objects, graphics, and movies. Presentation software often comes with a library of clip art from which the user can select graphic images to enhance the presentation.

The user can also find or create graphic images and export them into the software. By converting the presentation into PDF or flash animation formats, the user can display it more easily on the Internet.

Computer-Aided Design

Computer-Aided Design, or CAD, software supports engineers and other users as they design both real and virtual objects. It includes applications for creating shapes, curves, and surfaces in both two- and three-dimensional spaces. In addition to the design itself, CAD can display a wide array of figurative data, such as dimensions, tolerances, measurements, materials, and processes. Many industries rely heavily on CAD software. For instance, in the industrial arts, it is used to design cars, ships, and airplanes. CAD is also used to design prosthetics for the medical industry and building plans in architecture. In its virtual applications, CAD can generate documents, animation, and special effects for the movie and advertising industries.

Multimedia Software

Multimedia software allows users to combine a variety of media types (still images, text, audio, interactive applications, video, and animation) into a single presentation or document. Many industries make extensive use of multimedia software:

- Commercial – Engaging advertisements can enliven and sell products and ideas. Even communication inside the office or between organizations may require multimedia presentation.
- Entertainment and fine arts – Movie special effects, video game graphics, and interactive applications all make use of multimedia software. Art galleries often display works consisting of more than one media.
- Education – Many schools, especially universities, use multimedia presentations to enhance the learning process, such as computer-based training and edutainment.
- Engineering and scientific research – Computer simulations are used by engineers and scientists in various fields.
- Medical – Medical schools can train doctors through virtual surgery, which is a type of interactive application.

Interactive Multimedia Software

Interactive multimedia software displays a variety of materials (images, text, animation, videos, and audio recordings) based on the audience's interaction with the software. It also incorporates concepts such as interaction design and new media. The defining characteristic of this type of software is the mutual interaction between the program and its audience/end users—that is, both the audience and the program must react to each other's responses. There are many example of interactive multimedia software: video games, virtual reality, augmented reality social media, interactive television, interactive stories, ambient intelligence, and algorithmic art.

Communications Software

Communications software allows multiple computers to exchange files and messages—including text, images, audio, and video—remotely and over long distances. Examples include instant messengers, terminal emulators, gaming programs such as MUDs, file transfer programs, and network operating systems, which are highly complex. Modern communication software technology grew out of the bulletin board systems of the 1970s, which allowed text chat, and the terminal emulators of the 1980s. Even before the Internet rose to prominence, phone lines could transmit plain text messages between computers. Today, communication software enables groups of users to engage in chatting, which is a real-time exchange of information inside an Internet chatroom. In many cases, moderators oversee the chatroom, and prevent abusive behavior, such as spamming and flaming.

Groupware

Groupware is software that supports multiple users as they work together to achieve the same goal. It is also known as collaborative software, workgroup support systems, and group support systems.

Regardless of terminology used, its purpose is always enhancing collaborating by improving the manner in which documents and other media are shared and creating a collaborative working environment in which people help each other accomplish certain tasks. In business, common types of groupware include E-mail, video conferencing, application sharing, instant messaging, collaborative workspace, document management, task-flow management, and work-flow management. Using these systems, professionals can collaborate over long geographic distance. There are also many examples of groupware with non-business applications, such as Facebook, Twitter, Wikipedia, and various social networking services. Groupware is similar to computer supported cooperative work (CSCW).

Software Suites

A software suite, also known as an application suite, includes a bundle of several related programs, usually application or programming software. Vendors and software makers bundle these programs together and sell them at a single price. In most cases, each program in the suite offers similar user interface features and can easily export data between each other. Common types of software suites include offices suites, internet suites, and graphic suites. A graphics suite bundles together programs specifically related to creating and working with graphics, such as bitmap graphics editors, vector graphics editors, animation programs, and VRML editors. By purchasing them in a bundle, the user gets not only a cheaper price but also faster interaction time between the programs than if they were purchased separately. Common graphics suites include Adobe graphics, Corel graphics, and Microsoft Expression Studio.

Office Suites

An office suite, also known as a proprietary suite, includes a bundle of programs with a consistent user interface. In most cases, the programs can interact with each other at a much faster pace than if they had been purchased separately. Office suites are designed for use by knowledgeable users—that is, users with expertise in a certain subject area such as engineering, teaching, information technology, nursing, etc. Office suites often include word processors, desktop publishers, spreadsheet applications, graphics suites, end-user databases, speech recognition functions, presentation programs, communication (electronic mail, voice mail, and fax) functionality, electronic meeting systems, personal information managers, work group computing, notetaking programs, formula editors, analysis graphics and web log analysis software.

Personal Information Manager

A personal information manager, or PIM, supports the managing and organizing of personal information. It enables users to record and track notes and journal entries, addresses, important dates, appointments, meetings, reminders, alerts, project management, RSS/Atom feeds, E-mail archives, instant message archives, faxes, voicemails and lists. Multiple PIMs can connect over a computer network and exchange information.

Formula Editor

A formula editor simplifies the process of inserting mathematical expressions and formulas (such as fractions, radicals, superscripts, subscripts, arrows, symbols, etc) into documents. It enables users to publish technical data in both printed and electronic formats, and can also reformat equations into simplified forms. Formula editors acquire content from markup languages.

Web Log Analysis Software and Analysis Graphics

Web log analysis software, also known as a web log analyzer, uses certain indicators to determine information about web site visitation, such as how often the site is being visited, when it is being visited, and who is visiting. These indicators, which are based on the log files from web servers, include the following: number of site visits, number of site visitors, location of visitors, HTTP referrer, HTTP errors, search engine entries that led to the site, site pages with the most views, hosts lists, peak viewing times, browsers through which the site was accessed, the OS through which the site was accessed, robots, etc.

Analysis graphics is software that displays statistical information using graphic representations, such as charts and tables.

Internet Suite

An Internet suite provides a bundle of software programs that enable Internet access, such as a web browser, download manager, E-mail application, HTML editor, and IRC client. During the 1990s, web browser vendors sold suites on compact disk, creating much diversity and variety in available Internet software; however, due to various markets factors (such as the rise of AJAX web applications), the availability of Internet suites fell to only a couple options per year. Common Internet suites include the following: Mozilla (Firefox, Thunderbird, and Sunbird), Internet Explorer, Google Chrome, MSN Explorer, Opera, Netscape, Netscape Communicator, Arachne, Cyberdog, AOL Desktop, OmniWeb, and KDE's Konqueror.

CorelDRAW Graphics Suite and Microsoft Expression Studio

CorelDRAW graphics suite is a type of vector graphics editing software. It was created and sold by the Corel Corporation. CorelDRAW include the following software applications:

- CorelDRAW – is the vector graphics editor.
- Corel PHOTO-PAINT – offers various editing features, and supports Raster images.

- Corel CAPTURE – provides several methods of capturing images.
- Corel PowerTRACE – provides a means of converting raster images into vector graphics.

Microsoft Expression Studio is a graphics suite capable of creating web client applications, Windows client applications, and other rich digital media documents. It includes the following software applications:

- Microsoft Expression Web – helps design websites and edit HTML.
- Microsoft Expression Blend and SketchFlow – includes a visual interface builder.
- Microsoft Expression Design – helps edit raster and vector graphics.
- Microsoft Expression Media – manages digital assets.
- Microsoft Expression Encoder – encodes digital video for VC-1 and H.264/MPEG-4 AVC.

Information Systems Software Development

Systems Development

Systems development—also known as information system development or application development, or the "waterfall model"—is one of the most common software development methods. Its goal is creating an information system that solves a problem within the organization and whose cost does not exceed budget constraints. System development involves eight steps: systems investigation; feasibility studies; systems analysis; systems design; programming; testing; implementation; and, operation. Of all the software development methods, systems development is the most structured. The project team must complete one step entirely before moving to the next one, and progress is measured in terms of deliverables, such as requirement specifications, design documents, test plans, code reviews, etc. This structured approached has the advantage of keeping down costs. However, the disadvantage is a lack of flexibility and adaptability to problems that arise later in the development cycle.

The first three steps of the systems development method include the following:

1. System investigation - evaluates the proposed system and its implementation in terms of their cost-effectiveness. It then determines whether the project is a go or no go.
2. Feasibility studies - determine the preliminary information on the new system, such as the needs of its probable users, resource requirements, costs, and benefits. This step is also known as preliminary studies.
3. Systems analysis - involves setting parameters on the basic functions of the system. In this step, the development team identifies the business problem, researches the system or method that currently addresses the problem, and specifies the functional requirements of the proposed system.
4. Systems design - determines the methods by which the proposed systems will fulfill its functional requirements. These methods are known as the system specification, which include the following information: inputs, outputs, and user interfaces required by the system; hardware, software, networking, procedures, and personnel requirements for operating the system; and, integration of components and transactions within the system.
5. Programming - uses one or more programming languages to create computer code for the software that runs the system.
6. Testing - determines whether the code carries out the correct functions and meets system specifications.
7. Implementation - involves training users and converting data files from the old system to the new system.
8. Operation - places the new system into regular use.

The final task of the system development method is maintenance, in which the new system is monitored for previously undetected errors and any necessary changes or upgrades are made.

Software Prototyping

Software prototyping is a software development method that omits any feasibility or system specification study and, instead, creates a program based entirely on end-user requirements. This method includes the following steps:

1. Determine basic system requirements, such as required input and output.
2. Create an initial prototype that has only user interfaces.
3. Allow end-users to use their prototype and consider their feedback.
4. Improve prototype based on user feedback.

Software prototyping is most effective for developing small systems, user-interfaces for large systems, and online systems in which screen dialogue plays a prominent role. With these types of systems, designers can gather beneficial information from building an initial prototype and observing the proposed users as they interact with it. Prototyping is less beneficial for calculation-heavy functions, such as batch processing, which require little user interaction.

Rapid Application Development and Outsourcing

Rapid application development, or RAD, is a software development method in which a computer handles many of the responsibilities and functions associated with designing systems. RAD uses a software tool known as CASE, or Computer-Assisted Software Engineering, which is capable of diagramming, analyzing information, storing documents, generating documents, and writing code. In RAD, the development team engages in very little planning and, instead, goes to rapid prototyping. Any planning is integrated with writing the software—this approach decreased the length of time needed to design the system and facilitates any changes that may need to be made.

Outsourcing (in the context of software development) occurs when an organization hires an external party to design and create a system. Organizations outsource for a variety of reason: cheaper cost, lack of skilled labor such as an expert IT department, etc.

Object-Oriented Analysis and Design

Object-oriented analysis and design, or OOAD, is a software development method that relies on object-modeling. The software is designed using models of interacting objects, each of which represent a certain aspect of the system. An object has a unique type, data elements, and behaviors. The development team analyzes these objects in both their run-time deployment, and static and interacting states. Object-oriented analysis and object-oriented design describe two unique processes. The former uses object-modeling to determine the system's functional requirements, which are the tasks that a system is supposed to perform. The latter uses object-modeling to determine the system's specifications, which are the methods the software will use to carry out its functions.

System Development Tools

Gantt Chart, And Program Evaluation And Review Techniques

A Gantt chart illustrates the time requirements and tracking for every step in the systems development process. Each step is allocated a certain amount of time for completion. In most cases, each step is further divided into many different unique tasks (possibly hundreds), and each process will have a Gantt chart.

A program evaluation and review techniques, or PERT, chart also shows time allocation and tracking. However, it provides a more complex illustration by showing every task and their dependence on each other. Each task is represented by a node, and the nodes are connected to each other in a network. Certain tasks cannot be started until the prior task has been completed.

System Flowchart, and Data Flow Diagram

A system flowchart shows the logical arrangement of the various components that make up a system—specifically the files, inputs, outputs, and processing—with an emphasis on the hardware devices that the system operates Flowcharts are used most commonly during the systems design phase. In most cases, prior to the programming phase, the development team will create a unique flowchart for each process in the proposed system. For the sake of conformity and understanding, all flowcharts use the same symbols.

A data flow diagram illustrates the relation between the data produced by the system and various departmental groups.

Information Processing Methods

Batch processing is an information processing method that is common in computers with many users, such as mainframe computers. User interaction is not required to run the program; instead, the operating system executes the program after a user submits a batch request, and then alerts the user once execution is finished. The operating system schedules each batch request according to a set of priorities that have been programmed into it. The major advantage of batch processing is its high efficiency; when receiving multiple requests of the same type, it executes them together. Batch processing is not limited to mainframe and other large computers, however; it is also used by personal computers in many programs that require a great amount of information to be processed at once (such as a virus scan), and also gives the "batch" extension (.BAT) its name, in which a user can write a script of a set of actions to perform once the batch file is run. PCs use batch processing for routine functions that have no set time constraints—that is, they can be carried out whenever the necessary resources come available.

Real-time, sometimes known as online processing, is instantaneous; as the soon as the request is received, the operating system processes it. Consequently, the OS must have access to online random or direct access files.

Multiple program loading enables users to load more than one program at once even though the operating system only keeps one program active at any given time.

Multiprogramming is synonymous with multiple program loading.

Multiprocessing occurs when an operating systems executes multiple portions of a program at the same time. It requires a computer with multiple CPUs (or at least a CPU with multiple processing units, or cores) and an operating system that can perform parallel processing.

Multitasking occurs when an operating system executes multiple programs simultaneously. In most cases, a program that requires user interface is carried out in the foreground where a user can interact with it. Meanwhile, a program that does not require user interface processes information in the background. For example, as the user surfs the Internet, a printing of spooled output may be carried out in the background.

Fault tolerant computing enables an operating system to continue functioning properly where errors have occurred. It involves using redundant computer components, which overcome the errors to generate accurate data. Most of these redundant components are related to processing and memory.

Multithreading is a technology in which the processor is processing multiple tasks simultaneously. It is a type of multitasking. Normally, while multiple programs can be running at once, there is only one pipeline through which information is processed (and thus every program has to wait its turn in line, essentially). In multithreading, more than one set of instructions can be processed concurrently. An example of the importance of this technology is based upon the need to separate priorities and maintain performance—for instance, if a user were using a computer-aided design (CAD) program, rendering an image, and also needed to perform another critical task such as running a virus scan, these two intense processes would clash and thus take a very long time without the ability of the processor to handle multiple "threads."

Boot and System Support Programs

Boot describes the process by which the computer is made ready for use. The computer must first clear RAM memory and then load the operating system. Boots can be cold or warm. In a cold boot, the computer is simply powered on. In a warm boot (also known as a reboot), the user sends a request for a system restart, which allows the computer to shut down safely before restarting.

System support programs, also known as system utilities, perform helpful tasks, such as printing out files on a hard disk or generating a screen image. System utilities are part of a larger group of programs called system software.

Software Development Life Cycle

The software development life cycle describes the process by which computer systems are developed to solve business problems It is also known as the information systems or application development life cycle, and include the following phases: investigation, analysis, design, implementation, and maintenance.

Feasibility studies are part of the software development process. Although they are often performed in the investigation phase, they can be performed in any phase. The timing of the feasibility studies is entirely a matter of organizational preference. They include the following:

- Economic feasibility study – involves a cost/benefit analysis. The findings of this analysis determine whether or not the project will continue.
- Technical feasibility study – examines existing technology, and assesses whether it is sufficient to carry out the project.
- Operational feasibility study – analyzes the organization's managers and employees, and determines whether or not they will be capable of using the new system.

Investigation and Analysis

Investigation, also known as information systems planning, is the first phase of the software development life cycle. It often involves conducting strategic planning, which determines the overarching goals, strategies, and policies of the project, and operational planning, which establishes an operating budget for the project. An operating budget sets allowances for system maintenance, upgrades, and new projects. Additionally, during the investigation phase, the development team often performs studies on economic feasibility, technical feasibility, and operational feasibility.

Analysis is the second phase of the software development life cycle. Its purpose is identifying the problems in the current system, and determining the requirements of the new system. The development team divides the system into its separate components, creates diagrams and other analysis tools, and interviews users to determine their preferences. Using this information, the team creates goals and requirements.

Design

Design is the third phase of the software development life cycle. Its goal is creating detailed descriptions of the proposed system's functions and operations. At the beginning of the design phase, the development team examines the system requirements that were created during the analysis phase. Then, after conducting workshops and interviews and creating prototypes, the team creates design elements for each system requirement. Design elements are detailed descriptions of software features, such as functional hierarchy diagrams, business rules, screen layout diagrams, business process diagrams, pseudocode, and entity-relationship diagrams with full data dictionaries. The final output of the design phase is a full description of the new system using modules and subsystems. Programmers will use this description to create code for the new software.

Implementation and Maintenance

Implementation is the fourth phase of the software development life cycle. Using the descriptions (modules and subsystems) that were created in the design phase, programmers write the code that will carry out system functions. Once code is written for a certain module, developers must test it before it can be integrated into the main system. Testing does not always occur in the same phase; its timing varies based on the software development method being used. Types of tests include the following: performance testing, user acceptance testing, data set testing, unit testing, integration testing, regression testing, etc.

Maintenance is the fifth phase of the software development life cycle. After being put into operation, system performance must be monitored and corrected when errors arise. The system will likely require updates, and new users will need training.

Transaction Processing

Transaction processing, or TPS, helps businesses to track their transactions. Specifically, TPS performs order processing, general ledger, inventory management, payroll, accounts payable, account receivable, legal information management, and other functions related to transactions.

Online transaction processing, or OLTP, is a type of real-time processing. It provides immediate processing of transactions, and instantaneously updates files and databases without the need for sorting. OLTP requires extra software for security and error detection; otherwise, the system risks instantaneous data corruption. The likelihood of data corruption is too great without it.

CODASYL

CODASYL, also known as Conference on Data-Systems Language, was a professional standards organization. Its purpose was creating more efficient data systems analysis, design, and implementation, and developing a universal programming language that multiple computers could use. CODASYL had two major contributions: helping to develop and normalize COBOL language, and the standardization of database interfaces. Established in 1959, CODASYL was comprised of industry and government experts in information technology. It published computer language specifications which were adopted and used by ANSI, ISO, and other official standard bodies. One notable specification was the network database model, also known as the CODASYL model. This was written by the Data Base Task Group, or DBTG, which CODASYL formed in 1967. The network database model included multiple languages for defining schemas, updating databases, and requesting information from databases.

ANSI

ANSI, also known as American National Standards Institute, is a private, non-profit standards organization. Its purposes are overseeing the creation of industry standards for products, systems, services, and processes across the United States; accrediting organizations and professionals; and, coordinating those standards with other countries. Although membership is voluntary, ANSI consists of millions of professionals, and hundreds of thousands of companies, government agencies, academic institutions, and other organizations. These can receive ANSI accreditation by conforming to international standards. In the field of information technology, ANSI oversees the development of programming language standards. It makes certain that the terminology, testing methods, and product performance and features are uniform throughout the industry. ANSI does not develop standards; rather, it approves and accredits the standards and processes used by organizations.

IETF

The IETF, or Internet Engineering Task Force, is an open standards organization, meaning it has no formal membership. It creates and advocates standards for the Internet, specifically those related to the Internet Protocol Suite, and collaborates with other Internet standards organizations, such as WC3 and ISO/IEC. These standards are established through general consensus of its members. The IETF consists entirely of volunteers, who may be funded by a sponsor or organization. These volunteers are divided into working groups and informal discussion groups. Each group creates a charter, which details its purpose, and then performs work related to one of the following subject matter areas: applications, real-time applications, general, Internet, operations and management, routing, security, transport, and infrastructure. Once work is completed, the group disbands. As member of the Internet Society, the IETF follows certain legal and financial standards. The IETF publishes draft specifications and test results, focusing on individual protocols rather than entire systems. Consequently, these protocols have a applicability to a wide array of systems.

W3C

The W3C, or World Wide Web Consortium, is an international standards organization that ensures uniformity within the protocols and languages used by the World Wide Web. Before the W3C's inception, vendors offered different and sometimes incompatible versions of HTML. This created problems when navigating between web pages. Following the W3C's creation, vendors had a uniform set of standards and components from which to work, ensuring that each version of HTML was compatible with every other version. Whereas other standards organizations offer certification programs, the W3C does not. Although there are a number of standards and requirements for earning membership, the W3C can reject or approve an applicant for any reason. Only businesses, government agencies, nonprofit organizations, and universities can apply for membership. Individuals cannot. Any recommendation to the W3C passes through five phases before approval: working draft; last call working draft; candidate recommendation; proposed recommendation; and, W3C recommendation.

ISO/IEC

The ISO/IEC is an international standards organization that ensures uniformity in all types of information technology systems and tools. Established in 1987, the ISO/IEC was the product of a merger between ISO (International Organization for Standards) and EIC (International Electrotechnical Commission). Its goals are creating, maintaining, and advocating global IT standards that fulfill the needs of businesses and users. These needs include the following: standardizing the tools and components of IT technology, designing and implementing IT systems and tools, ensuring security within IT systems, maintaining high performance, creating portable systems, ensuring compatibility between two different systems, and designing user interfaces that are ergonomically sound and user friendly. Any national body can apply for membership in the ISO/IEC, and members are classified as either observing or participating—the latter can vote on proposals, and the former cannot.

Graphical User Interface

A graphical user interface, or GUI (commonly pronounced "goo-ey"), is common in modern interactive software. The user interacts with the software through icons, which are symbols that correspond to specific functions, tasks, and programs. Other common GUI components include dialogue boxes, pull-down menus, drop-down list boxes, scroll bars, navigation bars, radio buttons, and check boxes. Due to the complexity of GUIs, they require more processing power and memory to run effectively than their text-only predecessors, and as program design becomes more and more attractive with the advent of transparencies and high-resolution textures, these resource-needs will continue to grow. GUIs have their origins in the Xerox Corporation where researchers discovered that people identify icons and symbols more quickly and easily than they read words and text. Any GUI will attempt to incorporate ergonomic research into its design.

Ergonomics

Ergonomics, also known as "human factors," is the science of designing the workplace and all elements contained therein so they support rather than hinder worker health and productivity. Ergonomics focuses on improving the interaction between workers and their environment in order to enhance both their well-being and productivity. When a workplace element (such as a chair, keyboard or computer screen) is designed ergonomically, it will safeguard against repetitive strain injuries that can reduce a person's productivity and, more importantly, leave him disabled later in life. In addition to health issues, ergonomics is also concerned with designing interfaces that are intuitive for users. For instance, using keyboards with letters arranged alphabetically would not be an ergonomically appropriate decision because it would undermine years of training and force the worker to learn an entirely new method of typing.

Presentation Graphics

Presentation graphics allow the user to view and interact with information graphically rather than textually. This is useful for complex information, such as statistical data, which can be understood more easily when presented using graphical forms, such as line graphs, bar graphs, and pie charts. Using these forms, the audience is more likely to spot trends and patterns and, thereby, make good, well-informed decisions. Additionally, certain presentations may use audience response systems, which allow interaction between the audience and the presenter. Such systems include remote controls, web polls, telephone polls and any device that enables the user to give feedback. In classrooms, students can answer questions using personal response systems, which function like a clicker.

Hypermedia

Hypermedia is type of multimedia user interface. Multimedia presentations make use of text, graphics, voice clips, video clips, photographs, and other types of media. Through a hypermedia interface, users can access this media in whatever order they see fit using a hypertext system with hyperlinks. When users click on a hyperlink (the often-underlined text which links to another web resource), they access a new web page containing additional information and media. Hypertext describes the method by which the presentation material has been prepared and published—that is, users can access information at their own rate and direction. Hypertext systems give users complete control over their presentation experience, allowing them to view information in an order that has not been predetermined by the presenter.

Digital Video Interactive

Digital video interactive, or DVI, is a type of interactive video system, which is capable of processing images, text, audio, and video. Created in 1984, DVI was the first multimedia desktop software that ran on IBM-compatible personal computers. Originally, DVI was a DOS-based application that displayed full-screen and full-motion video, graphics, still images, and stereo audio. Content was stored on CD-ROM disks, and took advantage of the fact that DVI used data compression to store audio and video files before any similar application was doing so. The video compression scheme was known as a presentation level video, or PLV. Intel eventually acquired the rights to DVI, and used it to create the MMX instruction set included in Pentium processors.

Project Roles

Project managers shoulder the responsibility for the success or failure of a project. Their specific responsibility are outlined in the charter, but normally include the following: managing project work; overseeing the creation of project documentation; setting and communicating project policies and standards; and maintaining communication between all project members, including stakeholders, team member, and sponsors.

Functional managers are responsible for the administrative duties in a project. These include allocating resources and personnel and evaluating their work. Functional managers must collaborate closely with project managers.

Project sponsors provide funding to the project, and have power to resolve project disputes and make final decisions. In most cases, they are executives within the organization.

Key stakeholders include anyone with a vested interest in the project, such as sponsors and end users.

Project champions are normally experts in a certain area or industry. They normally have a great deal of technical knowledge but lack management authority. However, they are very important in earning credibility and garnering support for the project.

Team members are assigned specific tasks that carry the project to completion, such as planning, programming, implementation, monitoring, etc. Members should receive responsibilities that expand their skill set while not exceeding it to a great degree. For instance, a beginning programmer would not shoulder the responsibility of designing an entire system.

Project office teams manage and define project processes.

Project Functions

Document management records the changes that have been made to project files and the identity of the person who made the changes.

Project history is a detailed record of the actions that have been undertaken during the project. It helps protect the company against liability.

System organization keeps track of files and documents related to the project so that managers and team members can access any piece of information easily and quickly. This is the filing system for the project.

Scheduling identifies the task that must be performed, when it must be completed, and who is responsible for it. This information is usually on a calendar or list.

Time tracking tracks the amount of time a person has spent working on the project. This is useful for billing purposes.

Communication ensures that important messages are sent and received and that everyone is actively involved in the process.

Issue tracking records any issues or problems that managers and team members may have during the project lifetime.

SOFTWARE DEVELOPMENT TOOLS

A software development tool is an application that performs mundane programming tasks or simplifies programming tasks that involve complicated functions. There are four basic software development tools: compilers, debuggers, documentation generators, and integrated development environments.

A debugger facilitates the process of looking through lines of code and finding errors. Using a debugger, programmers can more easily examine variables within lines of code and unearth faulty instructions that cause problems in execution.

An integrated development environment, or IDE, allows multiple software development tools to operate in conjunction. Using an IDE interface, a programmer can move between multiple tools more easily.

A compiler is capable of translating a programming language into machine code, which can be executed by the system. As most developers cannot write directly in machine code (which would be extraordinarily inefficient), the compiler takes a high-level language and translates its instructions (which are essentially macros of machine code) into executable machine code, which is the only type of code the computer can natively read.

A documentation generator creates user guidelines and programming documentation by analyzing design data and application implementation. Specifically, it compiles screen data, forms, data flow diagrams, and source code files in a manner that is much quicker and more efficient than would otherwise be possible.

Programming Concepts and Data Management

Pseudocode

Pseudocode is code that is described in general terms, avoiding the syntax of a particular language, but allowing programmers to analyze and understand the logic behind a system specification before converting it into actual programming language, which is more specific and complex. Pseudocode is written between the system specification phase and the coding phase and uses the same algebraic symbols that other computer languages use. These include the following:

- '+'means add.
- '-' means subtract.
- '*' means multiply.
- '/' means divide.
- '**' means exponentiation, or raising a value to a certain power. This symbol may vary depending on the language being used.

Using these algebraic symbols, computers can process expressions by computing their results. Pseudocode uses three types of simple statements: sequence, decision branching, and repetition.

Operator Precedence

In the absence of parentheses, operator precedence determines the order in which a computer evaluates program expressions. This order, from highest to lowest, goes as follows:

1. Exponentiation, or numbers that have been raised to a certain power.
2. Multiplication or division in the order they appear from left to right.
3. Addition or subtraction in the order they appear from left to right.

When parentheses are present, they are evaluated before any other expression. The innermost parentheses are worked before the outermost parentheses, and the expressions inside a parenthesis are worked in the order of operator precedence.

For instance, consider the following expression:

- `A * (B - C)`

First, the computer would calculate `B - C` because it is contained within parenthesis. Then, it would multiply the resulting value by A.

Statements Used In Pseudocode

Pseudocode is written in simple statements that fall under three basic categories:

- Sequence – arranges a group of computations into an ordered series of commands. Sequences are established using the pseudocode statement SET.
- Decision branching – uses conditions, which are tests of the relationships between multiple variables. If the relationship is true, the computer will perform a certain sequence of events. If the relationship is false, the computer performs a difference sequence of events. Decision branching is a sequence using the pseudocode statement IF (followed by a condition)...THEN... ELSE...END IF.
- Repetition – instructs the computer to continue performing a certain action sequence as long as a condition is true, or sometimes for a pre-determined number of iterations. Once the condition is false, the computer moves to the next action sequence. Repetition is established using the pseudo code statement WHILE (followed by a condition)...END WHILE.

SET Statement

In pseudocode, the SET statement assigns values to variables. Consider the following examples:

```
SET X TO 5

SET Y TO 7

SET Z TO 9
```

X now equals 5; Y now equals 7; and, Z now equals 9. Assume the following statement is added after the above three:

```
SET Z TO Y – X
```

The value of Z now changes to 2. Assume the following statement is added to the above sequence:

```
SET Y TO Z ** 2
```

The value of Y is now 4 because Z was changed. The computer always executes the statement in the order they are written.

Comparisons And Logical Operators

In pseudocode, a condition statement will use symbols to instruct the computer to make certain comparisons. These symbols include the following:

- = prompts the computer to test if two values are equal.
- < prompts the computer to test if the left value is less than the right value.
- > prompts the computer to test if the left value is greater than the right value.
- >= prompts the computer to test if the left value is greater than or equal to the right value
- <= prompts the computer to test if the left value is less than or equal to the right value.
- <> prompts the computer to test if the left and right values are not equal

In addition to comparison symbols, condition statements often use the following logical operators:

- AND – indicates that both operators must be either true or false.
- OR – indicates that at least one operator must be either true or false.
- NOT – indicates that a true statement should be made false and a false statement should be made true

IF...THEN...ELSE...END IF Statement

IF...THEN...ELSE....END IF statements instruct the computer to engage in decision branching. A conditional statement will follow the initial IF clause. If the condition is true, the computer will carry out the statement sequence after the THEN clause. If the condition is false, the computer will skip the THEN clause and instead carry out the statement sequence after the ELSE clause. Once it has executed one of the clauses, the computer will move to the END IF statement. Consider the following example:

```
IF (X < Y) THEN

SET SMALLER TO X

ELSE

SET SMALLER TO Y

END IF

SET X TO 1

SET Y TO 2
```

If the X is less than Y, the computer will set the "smaller" variable to X. If X is not less than Y, the computer will set the "smaller" variable to Y. After one of the clauses is executed, the values of X and Y are set to 1 and 2, respectively.

WHILE LOOP

WHILE...END WHILE statements instruct the computer to perform a repetitive function. A conditional statement will follow the WHILE clause, and the loop will repeat until the statement is false. Consequently, during the course of a WHILE loop, a value must change; otherwise, the loop will repeat into infinity. Consider the following example:

```
SET X to 100

WHILE X > 20

SET X TO X - 30

END WHILE
```

Before entering the WHILE loop, X is given a value of 100. Each time through the loop, the value of X is reduced by 30. Once it is less than 20, the loop will end. The final value of X through this loop is 10.

Parallel Conversion and Pilot Conversion

Parallel conversion is a method of transferring data from an old, outdated system into a newer system. It involves using both systems, old and new, at the same time and then comparing their operation to find problems. Once the organization corrects any problems and determines that the new system meets all required specifications, the old system is deactivated. Parallel planning is very labor and time intensive, requiring extensive planning to execute properly.

Pilot conversion is another method of transferring data between old and new systems. It is common in large organizations with multiple departments or locations that operate with a high level of independence. Only one location adopts the new system initially. If it is successful, other locations will follow suit.

Phased Conversion and Plunge

Phased conversion is a method of transferring data from an old, outdated system into a newer system. Only certain parts of the new system are implemented initially, and only specific departments can use them. If these parts fulfill their intended functions, additional parts of the new system are brought online, replacing those same parts in the old system, and more departments are brought into the mix. If the implementation is successful, the new system will eventually replace the old system. Phased conversion occurs along a detail schedule with specific milestones.

Plunge is another method of transferring data between old and new systems. It involves implementing the new system as quickly as possible. The changeover is immediate, using none of the precautions of the other conversion methods—parallel, pilot, or phased.

Programming Methodology

Programming methodology describes the method by which software is coded and put together. Software consists of three basic components:

- Units of code – are written by programmers. These units determine the interfaces, screens, processes, storage files, and outputs that a software application produces. Once a unit is completed, it is tested. If it fulfills all its requirements, it and other units are grouped together into a module.
- Modules – consist of units of code. Each module is tested to ensure that all of its units can work together to perform their intended functions. If it passes the test, it is connected to other modules to form a subsystem.
- Subsystems – consist of modules. Each time a new module is added, the system is tested to identify any errors in execution.

Designing Vs Programming Software

When designing software, programmers begin with a set of generalized, high-level concepts and work their way down to the algorithms that make up the program. In this way, software design is a top-down process. First, programmers determine the functional requirements of the software. Second, they define the relationships between modules. Lastly, they design the algorithms. By contrast, programming software is a bottom-up process. Programmers begin by coding and testing each algorithm. These algorithms are then combined into modules, which are tested and connected into groups known as subsystems. Programmers test each subsystem before combining them into the final program. In order to create a testing protocol for the final program, programmers must document and analyze each step in the programming process.

ALGORITHM

An algorithm instructs the computer to carry out an individual task or function. It is the most basic unit of a software program. When writing algorithms, programmers must be very precise; any ambiguity in the language could lead to errors and undesired results. These errors include endless loops (infinite repetitions in the performing of a certain task, and consuming an infinite amount of resources). To avoid these errors, the programmer must specify the exact amount of resources and the specific length of time the computer should spend to complete the task. Algorithms are essentially logical and mathematical solutions to particular problems, solved in the particular programming language being used.

DATA TYPE

A data type describes a set of data values. Common data types include real numbers, Boolean variables, integers, characters, alphanumeric strings, and floating-point numbers. A data type also indicates all possible operations within a value set, all possible values within the set, and the storage method for the set. Data types also place constraints on the interpretation of data within a system and, thereby, enable the type system to evaluate the correctness of computer algorithms. All programming languages incorporate data types—though the terminology may differ between languages—and may permit programmers to create new data types with their own operations. In most cases, new data types combine characteristics of existing data types.

ABSTRACT DATA TYPE

An abstract data type, or ADT, is a data type whose definition remains constant between different programs. In essence, when one or more programming languages use an ADT, they will have similar semantics for it. Common ADTs include stacks, queues, priority queues, strings, containers, lists, deques, maps, multimaps, multisets, trees, and sets. ADTs are used to describe abstract algorithms in simple terms, assess data structures, categorize data structures, and provide formal descriptions for programming languages. Although they are mostly theoretical and conceptual constructs, ADTs do appear in formal specification language. They can be implemented in the form of modules that include procedures for ADT operation. As conceptual tools, ADTs are important in object-oriented programming languages.

STACK

One of the most common and simple abstract data types is a stack. Its name derives from a stack of trays, which serves as a metaphor for data retrieval. Each tray represents a data element. The last data saved goes to the top of the stack and, as a consequence, becomes the first data returned when the computer retrieves information. A stack is known as a "last in, first out" (LIFO) structure. Stack abstract data types perform two primary operations:

- Push – occurs when a new data element is added to the stack.
- Pop – occurs when the computer retrieves the data that was saved most recently.

Stacks can include any data type, including stings, integers, real number, pointers, and even other stacks. Because the operations of a stack are the same regardless of the programming language being used, it is considered an abstract data type.

QUEUE

A queue is one of the most common abstract data types. It functions like a checkout line: The first person in the line will be the first person to leave the line. Similarly, in a queue retrieval system, the computer returns the first data element that was entered into the system; consequently, a queue is known as a "first in, first out" (FIFO) structure. A queue performs the same two operations (push and pop) as a stack abstract data type (the only difference is the pop operator):

- Push – occurs when a new data element is added to the stack.
- Pop – occurs when the computer returns the first data element that was saved.

The verb associated with entering data into a queue is "to enqueue." Similarly, that which pertains to the process of returning data is "to dequeue."

ARRAY

An array is a type of data structure. It contains elements that are identified using two features: the name of the array, and the element's location within the array. Arrays can have any number of dimensions. The following example is a single dimension array:

ARY = [3,7,5,1]

The elements contained within this array are 3, 7, 4, and 1. If the system wanted to access one of them, it would identify both the name of the array (ARY) and the single integer that corresponds to the element's location, which is usually zero-based (that is, the counting of positions begins at zero, instead of one). For instance, ARY(0) accesses the 3 element; consequently, ARY(0) = 3. The other elements are accessed as follows: ARY(1) = 7, ARY(2) = 5, and ARY(3) = 1.

MULTIDIMENSIONAL ARRAY

A multidimensional array is a type of data structure that is more complex than a single array. When a system accesses elements within multidimensional arrays, it identifies them using the array name and an integer set. Consider the following multidimensional array:

[1 4 8]

ARY = [3 7 5]

[2 9 0]

The elements contained within the array are 1, 4, 8, 3, 7, 5, 2, 9, and 0. If the system wanted to access one of them, it would identify both the array name (ARY) and the two integers that correspond to the element's location. The first integer is the row of the data element, and the second integer is the column of data element. Once again, these tend to be zero-based. For instance, ARY(1,0) identifies the 3 data element; consequently, ARY (1,0) = 3. Other elements include ARY(0,0) = 1, ARY(2,1) = 9, and ARY(1,2) = 5.

VARIABLES

A variable is a single location that stores one value within a computer's memory. It allows a computer to store various types of data, such as numbers and characters, on a temporary basis.

The data contained within the variable is generally input into an algorithm, processed later in the algorithm, and used to generate output. Variables are classified under two broad categories:

- Global – can be read and modified through any part of the program; as such, they are in scope throughout the entire program.
- Local – are in scope throughout only part of the program. This part usually encompasses a function or subroutine, over which the local variable can be read and modified. If a local variable is not in scope, it cannot be accessed without the part of the program which has it in scope passing it explicitly to another part of the program, where it is re-created as another local variable.

Loop and Condition Loop

A loop instructs the computer to carry out the same set of instructions more than once. There are three types of loops: conditional, counted, and infinite.

A conditional loop compares variables against a defined condition and, if the condition is true, carries out the instructions within the loop. The computer will continue to perform the instructions as long as the condition is true, and will only stop once it becomes false. Conditional loops use the terms WHILE or UNTIL. Consider the following example:

```
        A = 10

WHILE A < 100

LOOP

A = A * 2

END LOOP
```

The loop will repeat four times. The value of A at the beginning of the final loop will be 80. After that, the value of A will be 160, and it will fail the condition.

Counted Loop and Infinite Loop

A counted loop executes a set of instructions a certain number of times by defining a counting variable prior to entering the loop. The counting variable determines how many times the instructions will be carried out. Counted loops often use the terms FOR and NEXT. Consider the following example:

```
FOR A = 1 to 10

        X = X / 2

        Y = Y * 2

        Z = (Z + 1) / 2

NEXT
```

The above counted loop will be carried out ten times.

An infinite loop (also known as an endless loop) has no means of ending itself. It executes a set of instruction until the computer is shut down or an error occurs. Consider the following example:

```
A = 5

WHILE A > 4

LOOP

A = A + 1

END LOOP
```

The above loop will never stop because the condition will always be true. Although infinite loops often occur due to error, they are sometimes intentional.

Logic Conditions

Computer algorithms perform tests on data, and then use the results of those tests to determine which instructions to perform. These tests are conducted using logic conditions, which compare the data to a constant or variable. Common logic conditions include the following:

- Equals is expressed as '=' or '= ='. This determines if the data is the same value as the constant or variable.
- Less than is expressed as '<'. This determines if the data is of lower value than the constant or variable.
- Greater than is expressed as '>'. This determines if the data is of greater value than the constant or variable.
- Not equals is expressed as '!=' or '<>'. This determines if the data is not the same value as the constant or variable.

Boolean Operators and Limitations on Data Testing

In addition to the common logic conditions, computer algorithms use Boolean operators (also known as logical operators) to perform more complex tests on data. Boolean operators include the following:

- And is expressed as '&&'.
- Not is expresses a '!'.
- Or is expressed as 'II'.

When a computer tests data against a constant or variable, both the data and the variable must be of the same data type. For instance, an integer can only be tested against another integer, and a character can only be compared against another character. In some cases, if the data and variable do not match, the programming language will convert them into the same type, usually according to their ASCII value.

IF Statements

Using IF statements, computers perform logic tests on data. IF statements have three basic variations: ELSE, ELSE IF, and CASE. Although the syntax of an IF statement varies between programming languages, it generally follows the same basic structure. Consider the following examples:

- IF X<Y, THEN A

Translation: If X is less than Y, perform action A.

- IF X!=Y, THEN A

Translation: If X does not equal Y, perform action A.

- IF X=Y && Y=Y, THEN A

Translation: If X equals Y and Y equals Y, perform action A.

- IF X<=Y, THEN A

Translation: If X is less than or equal to Y, perform action A.

- IF X=1 || Y=2, THEN A

Translation: If X equals 1 or Y equals 2, perform action A.

ELSE Statement and ELSE IF Statement

An ELSE statement is one variation on an IF statement. It instructs the computer to perform a secondary action if the logical test fails. Consider the following examples:

IF X<Y, THEN A ELSE B

Translation: If X is less than Y, perform function A. If X is not less than Y, perform action B.

An ELSE IF statement instructs the computer to perform a different logic test if the first logic test fails. Consider the following example:

IF X<Y, THEN A ELSE IF X=Y THEN B

Translation: If X is less than Y, perform action A. If X is not less than Y, determine if X equals Y (second logic test). If this is true, perform action B.

CASE Statement

A CASE statement (also known as a SELECT or SWITCH statement) is used when a logic test could produce multiple outcomes. It instructs the computer to perform a different action for each outcome:

CASE 1: A

CASE 2: B

CASE 3: C

Translation: If logic test 1 is true, perform action A. If logic test 2 is true, perform action B. If logic test 3 is true, perform action C.

For statements, CASE statements provide a means of simplifying ELSE IF statements. For instance, the above CASE statement is the same as the following ELSE IF statement:

IF (logic test 1) THEN A ELSE IF (logic test 2) THEN B ELSE IF (logic test 3) THEN C.

Machine, Symbolic, and Assembly Languages

Machine language is the native language of a particular processor architecture. Almost no one can write directly in machine language, as it requires extensive knowledge of internal processor directives, and the ability to memorize commands as binary (zero and one) commands.

Symbolic language is the general name for the alternative to writing in machine code—namely, all languages which replace the sequences of zeroes and ones with symbols and acronyms; that is, words that describe what action the programmer wishes to perform using the processor's capabilities.

Assembly language was the first type of symbolic language, named such because it assembled the defined acronyms into sequences of binary code (0s and 1s). When writing in an assembly language, the programmer must code every line of CPU instruction, meaning the ratio between a line of code in assembly language and a line of code in machine language is still one to one. Today, assembly language is used primarily for special purpose computer applications.

High Level Language

High level language has long replaced assembly language as the predominant programming language. High level languages possess a number of advantages over their forerunners:

- They do not require a one-to-one ratio between lines of programming code and lines of machine code.
- High level languages are separate from the instruction set of the CPU; consequently, they can be used on multiple types and models of CPU.
- A highly level language is similar to a natural language such as English, allowing the programmer to write code in a more intuitive way.

Once a program is coded in high level language, it must pass through a compiler, which translates into it machine language for the CPU. There are five categories of high level language: procedural, object-oriented, functional, declarative, and special.

Procedural Category of High Level Language

Procedural is a category of high level programming language. It instructs the computer to execute the code in the order it is written. There are several examples of procedural languages:

- FORTRAN or Formula Translation – was prominent in the late 1950s, and is still well-suited for programming applications in science and engineering.
- BASIC or Beginner's All-Purpose Symbolic Instruction Code – was available in 1964, and used mostly as a teaching tool. BASIC does not require a compiler; as a result; it saw a revival in the 1990s as a means of programming personal computers.
- COBOL or Common Business-Oriented Language – has been used since 1960s for business applications.
- Pascal – was a popular teaching language in the 1970s.
- C language – was created specifically for programming UNIX operating systems. It was developed in the early 1970s, and is still very popular as a general-purpose language.

Object-Oriented Category of High-Level Language

Object-oriented is a category of high-level programming language. In the object-oriented method, the programmer first defines objects and then assigns operations to those objects. Below are two examples of object-oriented languages:

1. C++ – is derived from C language, and is used for a variety of applications. There are three principles to C++ language:
   a. Encapsulation – the process of hiding information inside an object.
   b. Inheritance – the process of transferring properties between related objects.
   c. Polymorphism – the process of giving the same name to different processes. This is allowed as long as the processes exist in different classes of objects.
2. Java – is derived from C and C++ languages. There are two types of Java programs:
   a. Applications
   b. Applets – mini-programs. For instance, a web document may embed an applet, and then a browser runs the applet after it has downloaded.

Special Category of High Level Language

Special is a category of high level programming language. It includes any languages that cannot be classified under the other categories, such as the following:

- PERL or Practical Extraction and Report Language – is capable of scanning text files, extracting information from text files, creating reports, and performing many of the same functions as the C language. Like JavaScript, PERL is known as a scripting language because it can be interpreted, or "read" (like a script) by the computer. For instance, the Common Gateway Interface (CGI) uses PERL to create scripts that manage HTML output.
- SQL or Structured Query Language – allows user to interrogate a database and, thereby, extract information.
- HTML or HyperText Markup Language.

HTML

HTML, or HyperText Markup Language, is classified under the special category of high level programming language even though it is not an actual programming language. Using HTML, programmers can embed formatting instructions into a file. The browser then reads the instructions and uses them to display the file on a computer monitor. An HTML file generally begins with angle brackets (<>), which enclose the word HTML. This lets the browser know that it is an html document. The information enclosed within the angle brackets is known as a formatting tag. HTML files consist of a <head>, which identifies the title and browser parameters, and a <body>, which identifies the text and formatting tags. Between the <body>…</body> tags, the content of the document is laid out using the formatting capabilities of HTML.

Functional and Declarative

Functional is a category of high level programming language which includes a group of primitive functions. By combining these functions, a programmer can create new functions and programs. Functional languages are poorly suited for designing information systems, but have their benefits in the academic sphere. An example of a functional language is Lisp, which was made available in the early 1960s.

Declarative is another category of high level programming language. It uses formal logic to create new programs, and is also not suited to implementing information systems. Declarative languages differ from imperative languages in that declarative languages state known information and desired outcomes, and allow the machine to derive the process, whereas imperative languages describe explicitly how to solve a problem. Declarative languages are essential to artificial intelligence. An example of a declarative language is prolog, which was made available in the early 1970s.

Data Structure

A data structure contains a number of related variables. Using data structures, systems can process multiple variables at once. This ability is very useful when handling large amounts of data, such as customer lists, inventory lists, etc. Pseudocode allows the programmer to work with only one variable at a time, which has almost no practical value in modern information systems. Procedural programming languages can handle a limited number of advanced data structures, increasing their practicality. However, only database systems can support the most advanced data structures, which enable the real-time processing of information. A special type of data structure is an array. It stores data in a list where it can be accessed easily. All data in the array must be of the same type. Procedural languages such as C, C++, Java, FORTRAN and COBOL make extensive use of arrays.

Array, One-Dimensional Array, Two-Dimensional Array

An array stores data in a fixed-size sequence. Every element within the sequence must be of the same data type—i.e., an array must contain all integers or all characters or all alphanumeric strings. Using a subscript (also, index), the computer selects data from the array for processing. In most cases, the subscript uses a zero-based set of enumerated integers (i.e., 0, 1, 2, ... n) and moves through the array by addressing the desired index value of the array. For instance, in C:

```
float accounts[10];
```

...would create a 10-element array of floating-point (decimal) numbers called 'accounts', which could then be modified using the index values 0-9 (10 total). Therefore, if we wished to store the value 15.9 in the first index of the 'accounts' array:

```
accounts[0] = 15.9;
```

Like all variables, the computer's memory stores the array only as long as the program is running.

A one-dimensional array is an array with data aligned in a single row, like a list.

A two-dimensional array arranges data in multiple rows and columns.

Record

A record is one of the simplest data structures. It contains one or more data elements, and stores them in sequential positions in the computer's memory. In many cases, these elements are of completely different data types (i.e. integers, text, alphanumeric strings, or any other type of value). A record consists of a name and different fields. Each field holds a data element. For example, a record might store information on a house. Each field within the record would contain a different characteristic of the house—square footage, dimensions, lot size, cost, street address, construction, names of owners, and any other pertinent information. Expressing these elements requires different data types, both numeric and textual. A computer stores records within files on the hard drive, and cannot process them without accessing and reading them.

Files Processed By Procedural Languages

There are two types of files that procedural programming languages are capable of processing. Both are featured in mainframes that perform batch processing:

- Sequential files – are best suited for storing information that is processed routinely. The computer must access the entire file before it can process any of the records contained therein.
- Random files (also known as direct access file) – allows the computer to process any individual record without accessing the entire file. In order to access the record, the user must have a record key, which is normally a unique number or designation. An example is an invoice number or a shipping number.

Database

A database stores large quantities of information, all of which relate to a specific topic or subject. It also allows for easy retrieval and updating of stored information through software known as a database management system, or DBMS, which far exceeds the capacity and capabilities of other types of filing systems. It enables users to create, maintain, and use database contents and, in most cases, includes features for sorting information and the grouping of reports. A DBMS normally includes a data dictionary, which lists the names and descriptions of every data record type and the relationships between them. There are six primary types of database models: hierarchical, network, relational, distributed, object-oriented, and hypermedia. DBMSs are designed to work with each of these models.

Hierarchical Database Model

A hierarchical database model arranges information in the form of an upside down tree-like structure, much like a family tree (i.e. the lineage of many children can be traced back to a single parent). At the top of the hierarchy sits a general subject, such as the United States of America. This subject is then divided into a group of related topics, such as the individual states that comprise the USA. These topics can be further divided into even smaller topics, such as the counties in every state.

Subjuect ->Topic->Subtopic, etc

Hierarchical databases are often described as a one-to-many relationship because every data element can be traced back to a single, overarching topic. Additionally, all related data elements reside on the same level in the hierarchy. The hierarchical model is very useful for nesting information, and was used prominently in early databases; however, since then, it has become obsolete.

Network Database Model

A network database model is similar to the hierarchical model because the nodes at the top of the model branch out into multiple nodes at the bottom. However, unlike a hierarchical model, nodes at the bottom can connect to multiple nodes at the top. This allows the model to display many-to-many relationships, which are the redundant relationships between information.

A network model consists of two main parts: records and sets. Records contain fields of information related to a specific topic, and sets display the one-to-many (hierarchical) relationships between records. Although network models can handle more complex information than hierarchical models, they are still obsolete.

Relational Database Model

A relational model is the basis for modern database design. It represents database information in two-dimensional tables, and shows the relationship between those tables. A relational database model consists of three basic parts: relations, attributes, and domains. Relations are represented by tables with columns and rows. Each column has a name, which is known as an attribute, and defines a unique data element. Columns contain a set of values of the same type. These values are known as domains. Each row (also known as a tuple) represents a specific entity and all the values that define it. Rows are often identified using keys. Consider the following example:

Name of Person	Weig ht	Heig ht
Paul	150	5'10"
Duncan	170	6'
Gurney	155	5'7"

In reality, the hard disk does not store information in the form of two-dimensional tables; rather, these merely provide a conceptual understanding of the operations of a relational database.

Distributed Database Model, Object-Oriented Database Model, and Hypermedia Database Model

Distributed database models are a type of relational model. In a distributed database, information is spread out over multiple computers that are often separated by significant geographic distances.

The object-oriented database model derives from the object-oriented programming method and incorporates many of the same basic concepts, such as encapsulation and polymorphism. Object-oriented databases have five basic parts: objects, attributes, classes, methods, and messages.

A hypermedia database model (also known as a hypertext database model) contains data elements that define a wide variety of information, including text, graphics, sound, and video. Compared to more traditional databases, hypermedia databases possess far less structure between data elements.

Structured Query Language

Structured query language, or SQL (pronounced "sequel"), helps manage information within relational databases. Based on relational algebra, SQL allows the user to interrogate databases and extract information in the form of records. Additionally, it facilitates the process of updating information, changing schemas, and controlling access to data. SQL consists of the following elements:

- Clauses – the optional parts of statements.
- Expressions – generate values or tables containing information.
- Predicates – define the conditions that SQL will use when finding data.
- Queries – retrieve specific information from the database.
- Statements – influence schemas and information, and manage other aspects of database information retrieval.
- Insignificant white space – part of statements and queries, but is largely ignored by SQL.

Object-Oriented Programming Method

In the object-oriented programming (or OOP) method, programmers use objects as the basis for designing software applications. Objects are defined by both the data they contain and the relationships between them. There are ten basic concepts in OOP:

1. Class – describes the characteristics (attributes, fields, behaviors, etc.) of an object.
2. Object – an instance of the class. Whereas the class is a blueprint, the object is the created output of that blueprint, inheriting the qualities of the class, but can be further modified.
3. Instance – is one copy of an object. For example, if the office of US President were a class, then Ronald Reagan would be an instance (object) of the President class.
4. Method – a routine which belongs to an object or class. If Ronald Reagan cut taxes more thoroughly than many other presidents, then perhaps "CutTaxes" could be a method that belongs to the Ronald Reagan object.
5. Message passing – describes the methods by which objects communicate to other objects.
6. Inheritance – is the process by which classes impart their attributes to subclasses and objects. For instance, if Ronald Reagan (object instance) is a President (class), and all presidents can veto, then the "Veto" method is available to the Ronald Reagan object. This reduces redundancy.
7. Abstraction – is method simplifying and modeling programming problems.
8. Encapsulation – hides the functional details of a class. The "Veto" method might be complex, but only the person who writes it in the class needs to know exactly how it works. Others can use the method whenever they invoke the class, without having to understand how the class works, internally.
9. Polymorphism – allows classes and their subclasses to be handled in the same manner.
10. Decoupling – separates object interaction from its class.

Data Warehouse

A data warehouse facilitates the reporting and analysis of information and, thereby, aids the process of management decision making. Data warehouses use a relational database management system, but tend to store data differently than operational databases. Most data warehouses include tools for managing data dictionaries; retrieving, changing, and loading information into a repository; business intelligence; and managing metadata. There are three primary design methodologies in data warehousing:

- Bottom-up – initially creates data marts to analyze and report on business processes. The data marts are then connected to create the warehouse.
- Top-down – stores all organizational information in a centralized data warehouse. Data marts are then created to process information specific to a department.
- Hybrid – combines the speed advantage of a bottom-up design with the consistency advantage of the top-down design.

Data Mining

Data mining is a method of examining information and extracting trends or forecasts that had gone unnoticed beforehand. Data mining uses data warehouses and data marts as sources. It is very useful in marketing, scientific research, and surveillance. In most cases, data mining is not performed on all available data but, rather, a sampling of that data; consequently, the accuracy of the trend or forecast depends entirely on how well the sample represents the population as a whole. Data mining consists of four basic tasks:

- Classification – arranges data elements into groups that the user defines.
- Clustering – arranges data elements according similarity rather than predefined groups.
- Regression – models the data according to the function that is least error-prone.
- Association rule learning – examines different variables for any relationships between them.

Data Mart

A data mart is similar to a data warehouse but has a much narrower focus, concentrating on only one function or subject area. It analyzes information for the benefit of a specific department or group within an organization. Although data marts are generally used in concert with data warehouses, they are not the same. Data marts provide information that fulfills user needs. Conversely, data warehouses focus on information that already exists and the methods for storing and retrieving that information. In a bottom-up warehousing methodology, data marts are created and then connected to create a data warehouse.

In top-down warehousing methodology, all organizational information is first stored within a central warehouse and then data marts are created to extract and analyze information.

XML

XML, or Extensible Markup Language, provides a set of rules and specifications for the electronic encoding of documents, using open standards produced by W3C. XML is specifically designed to be used over the Internet in order to simplify, generalize, and increase the usability of web documents and services. RSS, Atom, SOAP, and XHTML are examples of XML-based formats, which have become the default language for most office productivity software, including Microsoft Office, iWork, and OpenOffice.org. XML uses the following constructs:

- Characters – comprise XML documents. All characters are taken from Unicode.
- Processor and application – The processor examines the markup, converts it into structured information, and then sends it to the applications.
- Markup and content – the two categories of characters that comprise an XML document. Markup is offset using chevrons ("<" and ">").
- Tags – surrounded by the aforementioned chevrons, tags identify the beginning, end, and empty-element elements in a document.
- Element – a logical component of the XML document that begins with a start-tag and ends with an end-tag.
- Attribute – a special type of markup containing a name/value pair.
- XML declaration – the information that precedes an XML document.

Electronic Document Management

An electronic document management (or EDM) system helps manage, track, and store electronic documents and images of paper documents. Like most document management systems, EDM has tools for storing data and metadata (e.g., the date when the data element was stored and the person who stored it); integrating data with other applications; filing, retrieving, indexing and distributing in certain formats; providing document security, workflow and versioning (i.e. checking the information in and out to users); collaboration between users and searching for specific files and folders. As part of enterprise content management, EDM has applications for digital asset management, document imaging, and records management.

Image processing occurs when a document image is captured, stored, processed, or retrieved. These images can contain numbers, text, graphics, photographs and even handwriting.

Web Design

The purpose of web design is creating a web site, which uses the Internet to deliver content to a user. This content is created in hypertext or hypermedia, and is accessed using a web browser. Web sites usually contain text and images. Using HTML/XHTML/XML tags, programmers can imbed various types of media—such as pictures, videos, and plug-ins—into web pages. There are four basic considerations when designing web pages:

- Content – the information contained in the page. It should relate to other information on the site, and fulfill the needs of the users.
- Usability – refers to the ease with which the site can be navigated and interfaced.
- Appearance – refers to the graphics and text layout of the page. It should be uniform throughout the site.
- Visibility – describes the ease with which the site can be found. Does it appear in search engines?

Hypertext

Hypertext describes text, images, and other types of media that are viewed on an electronic device, such as a computer monitor. Hypertext can be static (meaning the information contained in the document does not change) or dynamic (meaning the information changes in response to the user). Static hypertext is especially important in the realm of electronic books; however, it also applies to software and documents used to cross-reference data. Dynamic hypertext usually includes user interfaces, such as pull-down menus. Hypertext documents contain hyperlinks, which allow the user to access related information by pointing and clicking. Because hypertext is capable of interacting with and reading documents, it also provides a structure for extracting information from databases and, most famously, the World Wide Web. Using various software packages, users can create hypertext documents, but these are limited to containing text and only few types of graphics.

Hypermedia

Hypermedia simply expands the concept of hypertext. It uses hyperlinks to arrange multiple types of media (text, graphics, video, audio, etc.) into a non-linear presentation. In this way, hypermedia differs from multimedia, which arranges multiple types of media into a linear presentation. The most well-known example of hypermedia is the World Wide Web, which includes hyperlinks, text, images, and videos that can be navigated in any order. Electronic documents are the most common method of displaying hypermedia, usually though applications such as Web browsers, media players, and voice command browsers. Users can create hypermedia documents using Adobe Flash, Adobe Director and Macromedia Authorware. Databases can make use of hypermedia through applications such as Visual FoxPro and FilmMaker Developer.

Practice Test

Want to take this practice test in an online interactive format?
Check out the online resources page, which includes interactive practice questions and much more: **mometrix.com/resources719/clepinfosca**

1. Which type of office application software is best used for tracking an employee's expenses on a business trip?

a. Word processor.
b. Spreadsheet.
c. Database management system.
d. Presentation software.
e. Image editor.

2. Which type of office application software is best used for making and maintaining an internal department newsletter to be printed and posted on a bulletin board?

a. Word processor.
b. Spreadsheet.
c. Database management system.
d. Presentation software.
e. Image editor.

3. Which type of office application software is best used for keeping track of large amounts of data and generating reports on these data for training office employees in different departments, using various training materials?

a. Word processor.
b. Spreadsheet.
c. Database management system.
d. Presentation software.
e. Image editor.

4. Items that appear on the desktop of a computer that start applications in other locations on the computer are called:

a. Wallpaper.
b. Software.
c. Operating system application tools.
d. Shortcuts.
e. Recycle bin.

5. A file that is deleted from the computer ends up in the:

a. Wallpaper.
b. software.
c. operating system application tools.
d. shortcuts.
e. recycle bin.

6. The image that appears as background on the desktop, behind any running applications, is called the:

a. Wallpaper.
b. Software.
c. Operating system application tools.
d. Shortcuts.
e. Recycle bin.

7. All valid e-mail addresses must contain which of the following characters?

a. Space.
b. Ampersand (&).
c. Dot (.).
d. Exclamation point (!).
e. At sign (@).

8. A valid e-mail address cannot contain which of the following characters?

a. Space.
b. Ampersand (&).
c. Dot (.).
d. Exclamation point (!).
e. At sign (@).

9. Which of the following applications cannot be used to send and read e-mail?

a. Microsoft Outlook.
b. Google Chrome.
c. Terminal Window.
d. Windows Mail.
e. Spreadsheet.

10. Which of the following applications is not a web browser?

a. Internet Explorer.
b. Firefox.
c. Opera.
d. Browsezilla.
e. Safari.

11. When using a web browser, each address normally starts with the letters http. What does the "h" represent?

a. High.
b. Hyper.
c. Head.
d. Height.
e. Hydro.

12. A web browser browses the Internet with all of the following types of connections EXCEPT a:

a. Wireless connection.
b. Firewalled connection.
c. Proxy-server connection.
d. Stand-alone connection.
e. Direct connection.

13. To view web pages, the best protocol to use is:

a. http.
b. ftp.
c. nntp.
d. smtp.
e. www.

14. To transfer files, the best protocol to use is:

a. http.
b. ftp.
c. nntp.
d. smtp.
e. www.

15. To transfer e-mail messages, the best protocol to use is:

a. http.
b. ftp.
c. nntp.
d. smtp.
e. www.

16. A specialized system used to aid geographic mapping systems is called:

a. Geographic information system.
b. Business intelligence.
c. Decision support system.
d. Expert system.
e. Statistical analysis.

17. A specialized system used to help make high-level decisions based on complex business intelligence information is called:

a. Geographic information system.
b. Business intelligence.
c. Decision support system.
d. Expert system.
e. Statistical analysis.

18. A specialized system designed to ask questions, collect data, and provide a suggested solution, often with a specific degree of accuracy, is called:

a. Geographic information system.
b. Business intelligence.
c. Decision support system.
d. Expert system.
e. Statistical analysis.

19. Which of the following is the standard for electronic data interchange transfers from the American National Standard Institute?

a. IEEE
b. 802.11
c. X12
d. ACM
e. ASCII

20. Benefits of electronic data interchange include all of the following EXCEPT:

a. It is more accurate than traditional transaction processing.
b. It is faster than traditional transaction processing.
c. It uses fewer natural resources than traditional transaction processing.
d. It is more secure than traditional transaction processing.
e. It makes just-in-time processing more difficult and time-consuming.

21 The electronic data interchange work process includes all of the following steps EXCEPT:

a. Loading trucks in a service bay.
b. Sending completed documents over the network.
c. Printing case labels and universal product codes.
d. Receiving an order from the buyer over the Internet.
e. Creating shipping invoices.

22. To integrate data and processes of an organization into a single system, which of the following processes should be used?

a. ABX.
b. ERP.
c. CRM.
d. SCM.
e. PLM.

23. To build long-term relationships with business customers, which of the following processes should be used?

a. ABX.
b. ERP.
c. CRM.
d. SCM.
e. PLM.

24. To manage the supply network for a company, including all raw materials and goods needed to make a product or service, which of the following process should be used?

a. ABX.
b. ERP.
c. CRM.
d. SCM.
e. PLM.

25. A magnetic device internal to the computer that is used to store data is the:

a. Hard drive.
b. Internal modem card.
c. Network interface card.
d. Arithmetic-logical unit.
e. Central processing unit.

26. A computer device that is used to connect a computer to hubs, networks, and other computers is called the:

a. Hard drive.
b. Internal modem card.
c. Network interface card.
d. Arithmetic-logical unit.
e. Central processing unit.

27. The central part of a computer that is responsible for the main processing load is the:

a. Hard drive.
b. Internal modem card.
c. Network interface card.
d. Arithmetic-logical unit.
e. Central processing unit.

28. Which of the following is primarily a computer input device?

a. Keyboard.
b. Monitor.
c. Network interface card.
d. Central processing unit.
e. Internal expansion slot.

29. Which of the following is primarily a computer output device?

a. Keyboard.
b. Monitor.
c. Network interface card.
d. Central processing unit.
e. Internal expansion slot.

30. Which of the following is primarily a computer processing device?

a. Keyboard.
b. Monitor.
c. Network interface card.
d. Central processing unit.
e. Internal expansion slot.

31. Which of the following file endings most likely indicates an audio file?

a. tiff.
b. vbp.
c. txt.
d. cpp.
e. wav.

32. Which of the following file endings most likely indicates a text file?

a. tiff.
b. vbp.
c. txt.
d. cpp.
e. wav.

33. Which of the following file endings most likely indicates an image file?

a. tiff.
b. vbp.
c. txt.
d. cpp.
e. wav.

34. What type of computing is exemplified when one large computer is in charge of the processing and several small computers simply access the data?

a. Client/server.
b. Wide-area networking.
c. Large-computer processing.
d. Mainframe.
e. Internet computing.

35. What type of computing is exemplified when powerful PCs provide the computing power, while data are accessed on another computer?

a. Client/server.
b. Wide-area networking.
c. Large-computer processing.
d. Mainframe.
e. Internet computing.

36. A local-area network architecture includes all of the following EXCEPT:

a. Cat-5e cabling.
b. RJ-45 jacks.
c. Internal hard drives.
d. Network interface cards.
e. Hubs.

37. All of the following are operating systems EXCEPT:

a. Windows.
b. Linux.
c. Snow Leopard.
d. Penguin.
e. OS/2.

38. An operating system performs all of the following tasks EXCEPT:

a. An interface between the retailer and the consumer.
b. An interface between the user and the applications.
c. An interface between the applications and the hardware.
d. The management of resources.
e. A host of computer applications.

39. An operating system functions with all of the following parts EXCEPT:

a. A kernel.
b. A system program.
c. An application program.
d. A system library.
e. A central processing unit.

40. The standard used for wireless computer network communications is:

a. 802.1g
b. 802.11g.
c. 811g.
d. 811.5g.
e. 811.2g.

41. What is the primary limiting factor for communication distance when dealing with cellular technology?

a. A distance of 2 miles.
b. Local interference.
c. Line of sight.
d. Curvature of the earth.
e. Satellite distance and coverage.

42. All of the following devices rely on satellites to work correctly EXCEPT:

a. Global positioning systems.
b. Auto navigation systems.
c. Cellular phones.
d. Satellite phones.
e. Remote-location television signals.

43. Software development methodology includes all of the following EXCEPT:

a. Scrum.
b. Massive.
c. Extreme programming.
d. Unified process.
e. Rational unified process.

44. All of the following statements about Visual Basic are correct EXCEPT:

a. It is proprietary software developed and sold by Microsoft.
b. It is a learning tool, made to help beginning programmers learn how to program.
c. It is a compiler.
d. It is an interpreted language.
e. It works on any platform and operating system.

45. All of the following software development programs require a compiler to execute programs EXCEPT:

a. Cobol.
b. Pascal.
c. C++.
d. Assembly Language.
e. Java.

46. The last stage of the system development life cycle is:

a. Planning.
b. Design.
c. Programming.
d. Testing.
e. Maintenance.

47. The waterfall method of the system development life cycle is best described by which of the following statements?

a. It is a sequence of stages where each stage must be completed before starting the next stage.
b. It is a sequence of stages that repeats over and over again until the process is complete.
c. It involves creating a prototype that works, then developing the software.
d. It involves dividing the project into parts and building each part separately, then combining the parts.
e. It involves building proof of the concept, then modifying it as needed for the users.

48. All of the following are agile software development methods EXCEPT:

a. Crystal methods.
b. Dynamic systems development model.
c. Scrum.
d. The waterfall method.
e. Extreme programming.

49. Who is most likely to be responsible for the development of a project plan?

a. Project team.
b. Project manager.
c. Project sponsor.
d. Project stakeholders.
e. Steering committee.

50. In order for a project management process to be successful, vendors must provide:

a. Primary decision-making for the project plan.
b. Additional products and services to support the project.
c. Project decisions that will affect the user interface of the project.
d. Oversight and control of the project.
e. Task and technical leadership for the project.

51. All of the following are project management functions EXCEPT:

a. Organizational systems.
b. Document management.
c. Time tracking.
d. Server management.
e. Communications systems.

52. A system where all checks are deposited in order at the end of the day is an example of what type of processing?

a. Batch processing.
b. Real-time processing.
c. Interactive processing.
d. Online processing.
e. Master file processing.

53. Which of the following processing types would be most useful for processing information in an air control system, tracking aircraft in the air and on the ground?

a. Batch processing.
b. Real-time processing.
c. Interactive processing.
d. Online processing.
e. Master file processing.

54. Completing a transaction within a transaction processing system involves a collection of actions that must have all the following properties EXCEPT:

a. Atomicity.
b. Consistency.
c. Isolation.
d. Durability.
e. Malleability.

55. What is the maximum number of different fonts that can be used on one page of one software program application?

a. One.
b. Two.
c. Three.
d. Four.
e. No limit.

56. Which of the following symbols traditionally indicates to the user of a software application program that they are to type or provide information to the program?

a. Single apostrophe (').
b. Colon (:).
c. Semicolon (;).
d. Exclamation point (!).
e. Asterisk (*).

57. When using a software application program, what does an underlined letter typically represent?

a. A special character that needs emphasis by the user.
b. A starting point for the eye of the reader.
c. An indication of the first letter of a word in a new section.
d. An indication that the letter can be used as an access key.
e. Nothing special or standard as it has various meanings.

58. What type of error is generated when a symbol or instruction is typed incorrectly?

a. Syntax.
b. General protection.
c. Logic.
d. Spelling.
e. User-generated.

59. In typical programming languages, what does the line X = X + 1 mean?

a. This is not correct and will generate an error.
b. Add X to 1.
c. Add 1 to X, and the value is stored in the variable X.
d. The sum of X and 1 are calculated and displayed.
e. This is false as X is not equal to X + 1.

60. Which of the following statements best describes a pseudocode?

a. It is a false code.
b. It is a code that contains various syntax errors.
c. It is an example of sample instructions that are written to help write actual source codes.
d. It is a certain type of complied computer language.
e. It is a derivative of a P-code.

61. All of the following are logical operators EXCEPT:

a. NOT.
b. AND.
c. OR.
d. XOR.
e. BUT.

62. Under what condition will the following code print hello?

```
If (A > 6), then
If (B < 7), then
Print nothing
Else
Print hello
Else
Print goodbye
```

a. When A is 6 and B is not 7.
b. When A is 10 and B is 2.
c. When A is 5 and B is 1.
d. When A is 10 and B is 10.
e. Under none of the listed conditions.

63. Using the binary number system, what is 1 + 1 + 1?

a. 3.
b. 111.
c. 101.
d. 11.
e. 100.

64. In object-oriented programming, what is a class?

a. A blueprint of an item.
b. The variable where the data are stored.
c. Any "thing" in the program that has methods, properties, events, and data.
d. A location in memory.
e. A value, usually true or false.

65. When defining a class, what type of function is executed when an object is instantiated?

a. Constructor.
b. Initial.
c. First.
d. Instantiated.
e. Mutator.

66. A function that is polymorphic when related to object oriented is one that:

a. Changes as the program runs.
b. Has different behavior, depending on the input to the function.
c. Is different for each instance of the class.
d. Changes location in memory, depending on the number of objects.
e. Works differently when called from different functions.

67. A data type primarily defines:

a. What a user can input into a text box.
b. Whether a user can input symbols in the data entry form.
c. The amount of memory reserved.
d. The format of the data as it will appear on reports.
e. Which keys on the keyboard will be accepted as input.

68. A structure, in programming languages, is used to store what type of information?

a. Meta data (data about the data to be stored).
b. Numerous parts of one type of data.
c. Just one type of data, stored in a specific layout.
d. More than one type of data.
e. Memory addresses (pointers).

69. What is the programming process called when a space in memory is reserved for a variable?

a. Instantiation.
b. Reserving.
c. Initializing.
d. Decrementing.
e. Incrementing.

70. A random access file is most similar to which of the following in terms of accessing records?

a. A tape deck.
b. A compact disc player.
c. A four-drawer file cabinet.
d. A paper file folder.
e. Raindrops.

71. What meaning does the three-letter file extension on file names have?

a. It determines what program created the file.
b. It helps determine which program should open the file.
c. It is determined by the operating system.
d. It is determined by the disk file system.
e. It has no purpose other than identification of the file by the user.

72. A flat file (sequential access) is most useful when:

a. The entire file will be read every time it is accessed.
b. The file stores large amounts of data.
c. The file is read and written numerous times throughout the day.
d. The file stores a very small amount of information.
e. There is a small amount of free space left on the hard drive.

73. The primary components of a database management system include all of the following EXCEPT:

a. A disc storage system.
b. A modeling language.
c. Data structures.
d. A query language.
e. A transaction mechanism.

74. Types of databases include all of the following EXCEPT:

a. Relational.
b. Transferring.
c. Object oriented.
d. Online analytical process.
e. Flat-file.

75. Database management systems include all of the following EXCEPT:

a. Microsoft Access.
b. IBM DB2.
c. Debian Linux.
d. MySQL.
e. Oracle.

76. In the following SQL statement, what information is needed to fill in the blank?

SELECT ____ FROM tbl_One;

a. Table names.
b. Column names.
c. Row numbers.
d. Information about the number of rows to be returned.
e. Nothing.

77. The following SQL statement will return how many rows?

Tbl_One Contents:

ID	Name	Department
1	Joe	16A
2	Fred	16A
3	Sally	12B
4	Tim	16B
5	Judy	12A

SELECT ID FROM Tbl_One
WHERE Department like '16?';

a. None.
b. One.
c. Two.
d. Three.
e. Five.

78. When joining tables in an SQL statement, in which part of the SQL statement should the manual join appear?

a. Select.
b. From.
c. Where.
d. Order by.
e. Table join.

79. The basic, standard language understood by all web browsers is:

a. HTML.
b. XML.
c. XHTML.
d. DHTML.
e. TMLH.

80. A web technology that has been expanded to make pages dynamic is:

a. DHTML.
b. Visual Basic.
c. W3C.
d. HTML.
e. Apache.

81. Programming languages used in web pages include all of the following EXCEPT:

a. PHP.
b. JavaScript.
c. ASP.
d. Assembly language.
e. Cold fusion.

82. Task types for data mining include all of the following EXCEPT:

a. Classification.
b. Clustering.
c. Rule learning.
d. Regression.
e. Storage.

83. Likely subjects for data warehousing include all of the following EXCEPT:

a. Wedding planning.
b. Credit card analysis.
c. Insurance fraud.
d. Federal law enforcement records.
e. Help desk call analysis.

84. Given enough data, all of the following statements can be predicted with some accuracy by data mining EXCEPT the:

a. Amount of sales a Boston store will generate next month.
b. Total number of books that have been sold through Amazon.com.
c. Number of people who will drive through a red light at a specific intersection.
d. Number of six-packs of beer that will be sold next Friday at one location.
e. Final score of the Saints–Dolphins game on Sunday.

85. Which amendment to the US Constitution asserts the right to privacy?

a. First.
b. Second.
c. Third.
d. Fifth.
e. None.

86. When using the Internet, which of the following methods commonly encrypt and secure data in transmission?

a. SSL.
b. HTML.
c. PHP.
d. TTL.
e. ISP.

87. Which of the following statements best defines a computer cookie?

a. It is a special reward that is given to the user.
b. It is a small file on a computer disc.
c. It is part of a larger program on a computer.
d. It is part of the Internet.
e. It is a slang term for parts of a web page.

88. Open-source software has which of the following qualities?

a. It is created by a company and then released to individuals for free.
b. It requires user registration before the software can be used.
c. It has no secret code and can be modified by the user.
d. It is sold by Microsoft and other large companies.
e. It does not really exist; it is just an outline of what someone would like to see.

89. Open-source software programs include all the following EXCEPT:

a. Open Office.
b. Apache.
c. Tomcat.
d. Microsoft Office.
e. Linux.

90. Computer software is protected by:

a. Copyright laws.
b. Patents.
c. Trademarks.
d. Service marks.
e. Privacy laws.

91. Ergonomics is the study of:

a. Computer operating systems.
b. File system layouts.
c. Work system layouts that conform to the human body.
d. Object database theory.
e. Fourth-generation languages.

92. Carpal tunnel injuries occur in the:

a. Eyes.
b. Head.
c. Shoulders.
d. Back.
e. Wrists.

93. The best definition of telecommuting is:

a. The study of telephones and communications.
b. Using computers to work from home or other remote locations.
c. Using remote computer devices, such as the global positioning system, in the car.
d. Using a car that is controlled by a computer.
e. Any job that involves the use of computers.

94. The best definition of a technical writer is one who writes:

a. Computer codes for application programs.
b. Instruction manuals for computer programmers.
c. Information for books on computers.
d. Technical information in nontechnical terms.
e. By telecommuting.

95. Responsibilities of a computer forensic technician include:

a. Recording and storing evidence for law enforcement agencies.
b. Working with computers that are dead.
c. Exploring computers and operating systems for errors and problems.
d. Those of an entry level computer programmer.
e. Instructing people in the ways that computers and networks work together.

96. True statements about a computer technical support position include all of the following EXCEPT:

a. It is an entry-level position that can lead to other career paths in computers.
b. It requires a great deal of experience and training.
c. There are various levels of technical support that require different amounts of knowledge.
d. A+ certification matches the skills needed for this position.
e. It includes network and desktop positions.

97. What type of program installed on a personal computer stops malicious programs from attacking that computer?

a. Virus program.
b. Spyware program.
c. Antivirus program.
d. Application program.
e. E-mail program.

98. The most common way that a virus spreads is through:

a. Open-network connections.
b. Unsecured computers and holes in firewalls.
c. Passing and sharing of disks and drives.
d. Opening e-mail attachments.
e. Using Internet web browsers.

99. Identity theft is best defined as:

a. The process of securing personal data on your computer.
b. When you lose your driver's license.
c. When a program attacks your computer and deletes files from your computer.
d. When passwords and user names are stolen to access your bank accounts.
e. When a person steals information about another and uses that information fraudulently.

100. Examples of outsourcing include all of the following EXCEPT:

a. The process of buying materials or software from a different department in your company.
b. Buying office supplies from the local office supply company.
c. Contracting with another company or person to complete a task.
d. Having sections of computer codes written by programmers in a foreign country.
e. Obtaining prewritten software instead of writing the software in-house.

Answers and Explanations

1. B: Spreadsheet. Spreadsheet software is designed to do calculations and reports based on numerical calculations. The word processor software is used primarily for documents that include large amounts of text, such as memos and newsletters. Database management system software is used to track data and generate reports. Presentation software is used to show data to a group of people. An image editor is used to process, change, and edit graphical files.

2. A: Word processor. The word processor software is designed to process large amounts of text and enable the user to format and layout the text in a way that provides for detailed printing. Spreadsheet software is used for calculations and reporting on the calculations. Database management software is used to track data and generate reports on these data. Presentation software is designed to show data to a group of people. An image editor is used to process, change, and edit graphical files.

3. C: Database management system. Database management system software is designed to track large amounts of data and generate reports based on these data. Word processing software is designed to layout and format text. Spreadsheets are used to do mathematical calculations and reports based on these calculations. Presentation software is used to show data to a group of people. An image editor is used to process, change, and edit graphical files.

4. D: Shortcuts. Shortcuts appear on the desktop to allow the user easy access to start an application. These shortcuts can be added to and removed from the desktop without actually adding or removing the application on the computer. Wallpaper is the image that appears on the background of the desktop. These images can be selected from those provided with the operating system or can be downloaded to the computer to be used as wallpaper. Software describes any of the computer codes that are stored on the disc, such as applications and the operating system. The recycle bin stores applications and files that have been deleted so the user can restore them if the deletion was accidental; however, once the recycle bin has been emptied, the files are gone forever.

5. E: Recycle bin. The recycle bin stores applications and files that have been deleted so the user can restore them if the deletion was accidental; however, once the recycle bin has been emptied, the files are gone forever. Wallpaper is the image that appears on the background of the desktop. These images can be selected from those provided with the operating system or can be downloaded to the computer to be used as wallpaper. Software describes any of the computer codes that are stored on the disc, such as applications and the operating system. Shortcuts appear on the desktop to allow the user easy access to start an application. These shortcuts can be added to and removed from the desktop without actually adding or removing the application on the computer.

6. A: Wallpaper. Wallpaper is the image that appears on the background of the desktop. These images can be selected from those provided with the operating system or can be download to the computer to be used as wallpaper. Software describes any of the computer codes that are stored on the disc, such as applications and the operating system. Shortcuts allow the user easy access to start an application. These shortcuts can be added to and removed from the desktop without actually adding or removing the application on the computer. The recycle bin stores applications and files that have been deleted so the user can restore them if the deletion was accidental; however, once the recycle bin has been emptied, the files are gone forever.

7. E: @ sign. The @ sign is required in all e-mail addresses as part of the format for the e-mail address. This sign helps the Internet and mail processing computers to understand where to send the e-mail. The part after the @ sign is the address of the computer that is the destination for the e-mail. The ampersand and explanation point can be included in e-mail addresses, but they are not commonly used. A dot is commonly used in e-mail addresses but is not required.

8. A: Space. A space is not allowed in any e-mail addresses. With Internet and mail processing computers, the space has a special meaning, but no e-mail address can contain a space. The ampersand and explanation point can be included in e-mail addresses, but they are not commonly used. A dot is commonly used in e-mail addresses but is not required. The @ sign is required in all e-mail addresses.

9. E: Spreadsheet. Spreadsheet applications are designed to do calculations and reports based on numerical calculations. Microsoft Outlook is the standard Microsoft application that is used to send and receive e-mail. Google Chrome is a web browser that allows you to browse the web and obtain e-mail via the Internet. A terminal window can be used to connect to an e-mail server and access e-mail accounts. Windows Mail is the application that is supplied with the Vista Operating System that is designed to send and receive e-mail.

10. D: Browsezilla. Browsezilla does not actually exist. Internet Explorer is Microsoft's version of the web browser. Firefox and Opera are popular open-source web browsers. Safari is the web browser used with Apple computers.

11. B: Hypertext. The http represents hypertext transfer protocol used by most web browsers. The web browser has been instructed to use this protocol for a particular operation. There are other protocols available for use by web browser (e.g., ftp, news), but http is by far the most common.

12. D: Stand-alone connection. A stand-alone connection is not actually a connection type but represents a computer that is not connected via a network to any other computer or device. Any computer that is not connected to anything is incapable of browsing the Internet. A wireless connection uses a wireless signal and an antenna to connect to another computer that is connected to the Internet, granting access to the initial computer. A firewalled computer is one that is connected to another computer, a firewall that provides limited access to the Internet. A proxy-server connected computer connects to another machine, a proxy server, which provides access to the Internet. A direct connection is a computer that is connected via a hub, router, or other device, directly to the Internet.

13. A: http. The hypertext transfer protocol, or http, is the primary protocol used on the Internet to view web pages that are encoded, using HTML language. The file transfer protocol, or ftp, is a protocol used to transfer files of all sizes through networks and the Internet. The network news transfer protocol, or nntp, is a protocol used to transfer news and information through Internet newsgroups. The simple mail transfer protocol, or smtp, is the primary protocol used across the Internet for transferring e-mail files. The world wide web, or www, is not actually a protocol with which to do anything on the web; it simply identifies the world wide web.

14. B: ftp. The file transfer protocol, or ftp, is the protocol used to transfer files of all sizes through networks and the Internet. The hypertext transfer protocol, or http, is the primary protocol used on the Internet to view web pages that are encoded, using HTML language. The network news transfer protocol, or nntp, is a protocol used to transfer news and information through Internet newsgroups. The simple mail transfer protocol, or smtp, is the primary protocol used across the Internet for transferring e-mail files. The World Wide Web, or www, and is not actually a protocol with which to do anything on the web; it simply identifies the world wide web.

15. D: smtp. The simple mail transfer protocol, or smtp, is the primary protocol used across the Internet for transferring e-mail files. The hypertext transfer protocol, or http, is the primary protocol used on the Internet to view web pages that are encoded, using HTML language. The file transfer protocol, or ftp, is the protocol used to transfer files of all sizes through networks and the Internet. The network news transfer protocol, or nntp, is a protocol used to transfer news and information through Internet newsgroups. The world wide web, or www, is not actually a protocol with which to do anything on the web; it simply identifies the world wide web.

16. A: Geographic information system. The geographic information system is designed to work with geographic data, including maps and related information. Business intelligence represents data that are collected and analyzed to aid in business planning. The decision support system is configured to make high-level business decisions based on large amounts of business data. An expert system is an artificial intelligence system that is designed to take the place of an expert in a specific field. This system collects data based on responses to questions and attempts to determine the best solution, just as an expert would. Statistical analysis is simply the process of analyzing statistics.

17. C: Decision support system. The decision support system is a complex specialized system that is configured to make high-level business decisions based on large amounts of business data. The geographic information system is designed to work with geographic data, including maps and related information. Business intelligence represents data that are collected and analyzed to aid in business planning. An expert system is an artificial intelligence system that is designed to take the place of an expert in a specific field. This system collects data based on responses to questions and attempts to determine the best solution, just as an expert would. Statistical analysis is simply the process of analyzing statistics.

18. D: Expert system. An expert system is an artificial intelligence system designed to take the place of an expert in a specific field. This system collects data based on responses to questions and attempts to determine the best solution, just as an expert would. The geographic information system is designed to work with various types of geographic data, including maps and related information. Business intelligence represents data that are collected and analyzed to aid in business planning. The decision support system is a complex specialized system that is configured to make high-level business decisions based on large amounts of business data. Statistical analysis is simply the process of analyzing statistics.

19. C: X12. The X12 is a set of standards approved by the American National Standard Institute (ANSI) to enable electronic data interchange transfers from one company to another. The Institute for Electrical and Electronic Engineers (IEEE) is an organization that is not related to ANSI. The standards developed by IEEE, 802.11, are used to determine how to undertake wireless communication between computers. The Association for Computing Machinery (ACM) is not affiliated with ANSI. The American Standard Code for Information Interchange (ASCII) is a set of definitions for character sets developed by ANSI.

20. E: It makes just-in-time processing more difficult and time-consuming. In fact, electronic data interchange makes just-in-time processing much simpler and faster. It is also more accurate, faster, uses fewer natural resources, and is more secure than traditional transaction processing.

21. A: Loading trucks in a service bay. The steps typical of an electronic data interchange process include the following: (1) The buyer sends an order to a company. (2) The company receives the order electronically and then sets up orders by the case, printing labels for the cases and creating shipping notices and invoices. (3) The company, as a last step, sends all related documents across the network to various different computers.

22. B: ERP. Enterprise resource planning (ERP) is a way to integrate data and processes of an organization into a single system. The acronyms ABX and PLM do not stand for anything. Customer relationship management (CRM) is a process by which to build long-term relationships with business customers. Supply change management (SCM) is a process by which to manage the supply network for a company, including all raw materials and goods needed to make a product or service.

23. C: CRM. Customer relationship management (CRM) is a process by which to build long-term relationships with business customers. The acronyms ABX and PLM do not stand for anything. Enterprise resource planning (ERP) is a way to integrate data and processes of an organization into a single system. Supply change management (SCM) is a process by which to manage the supply network for a company, including all raw materials and goods needed to make a product or service.

24. D: SCM. Supply change management (SCM) is a process to by which to manage the supply network for a company, including all raw materials and goods needed to make a product or service. The acronyms ABX and PLM do not stand for anything. Enterprise resource planning (ERP) is a way to integrate data and processes of an organization into a single system. Customer relationship management (CRM) is a process by which to build long-term relationships with business customers.

25. A: Hard drive. The hard drive is the primary repository for data storage inside the computer. These drives are magnetic and store and retrieve data, using tiny magnets and platters of material that respond to the magnets. An internal modem is a device inside a computer that can connect to standard phone lines for communication with other computers or devices. These are analog signals only. A network interface card usually includes an RJ-45 port that can connect to other computers and devices. An arithmetic-logical unit does complex calculations inside the computer, in conjunction with the central processing unit, and is responsible for the primary workload inside the computer.

26. C: Network interface card. A network interface card usually includes an RJ-45 port that can connect to other computers and devices. The hard drive is the primary repository for data storage inside the computer. These drives are magnetic and store and retrieve data, using tiny magnets and platters of material that respond to the magnets. An internal modem is a device that is inserted inside a computer that can connect to standard phone lines for communication with other computers or devices. These are analog signals only. An arithmetic-logical unit does complex calculations inside the computer, in conjunction with the central processing unit (CPU). The CPU is responsible for the primary workload inside the computer.

27. E: Central processing unit. The central processing unit (CPU) is responsible for the primary workload inside the computer. The hard drive is the primary repository for data storage inside the computer. These drives are magnetic and store and retrieve data, using tiny magnets and platters of material that respond to the magnets. An internal modem is a device that is inserted inside a computer that can connect to standard phone lines for communication with other computers or devices. These are analog signals only. A network interface card usually includes an RJ-45 port that can connect to other computers and devices. An arithmetic-logical unit does complex calculations inside the computer in conjunction with the CPU.

28. A: Keyboard. A keyboard is usually the primary input device for the computer unit. While a monitor, such as a touch-screen, can be an input device, it is used primarily to display output. A network interface card is a device that connects the computer to a network. It is used as an input and output device, depending on the needs of the computer and the user. The central processing unit, or the brains of the computer, does nearly all of the processing for the computer unit. An internal expansion slot is used to add expansion cards inside the computer and can be used for input, output, or absolutely nothing, depending on the needs of the computer.

29. B: Monitor. While a monitor is used primarily to display output, in some cases, such as a touch-screen, it can also be an input device. A keyboard is the primary input device for the computer unit. A network interface card is a device that connects the computer to a network. It is used as an input and output device, depending on the needs of the computer and the user. The central processing unit, or the brains of the computer, does nearly all of the processing for the computer unit. An internal expansion slot is used to add expansion cards inside the computer and can be used for input, output, or absolutely nothing, depending on the needs of the computer.

30. D: Central processing unit. The central processing unit, or the brains of the computer, does nearly all of the processing for the computer unit. A keyboard is usually the primary input device for the computer unit. A monitor is used primarily to display output, but in some cases, such as a touch-screen, it can also be used as an input device. A network interface card is a device that connects the computer to a network. It is used as an input and output device, depending on the needs of the computer and the user. An internal expansion slot is used to add expansion cards inside the computer and can be used for input, output, or absolutely nothing, depending on the needs of the computer.

31. E: Wav. Waveform audio format files, or wav, store any sort of audio information. A tagged image file format, or tiff, is a specific file format that is used for saving any kind of image, including photographs and computer drawings. A visual basic project file, or vbp, is the result of Microsoft's Visual Basic language programs. A text file, or txt, is a simple file format that contains just characters from the American Standard Code for Information Interchange. A C++ source file, or cpp, is usually a plain text file, but it is prepared to be processed by a C++ compiler program.

32. C: Txt. A text file, or txt, is a simple file format that just contains characters from the American Standard Code for Information Interchange. A tagged image file format, or tiff, is a specific file format that is used for saving any kind of image, including photographs and computer drawings. A visual basic project file, or vbp, is the result of Microsoft's Visual Basic language programs. A C++ source file, or cpp, is usually a plain text file, but it is prepared to be processed by a C++ compiler program. Waveform audio format files, or wav, are files that store any sort of audio information.

33. A: Tiff. A tagged image file format, or tiff, is a specific file format that is used for saving any kind of image, including photographs and computer drawings. A visual basic project file, or vbp, is the result of Microsoft's Visual Basic language programs. A text file, or txt, is a simple file format that just contains characters from the American Standard Code for Information Interchange. A C++ source file, or cpp, is usually a plain text file, but it is prepared to be processed by a C++ compiler program. Waveform audio format files, or wav, are files that store any sort of audio information.

34. D: Mainframe. Mainframe computers are computers that are set up to take the computer processing load but may be connected to several small computers, such as dumb terminals. Client/server computing is the process in which one computer, the client, provides the processing power, while another computer, the server, provides the data and information for the client. Wide-area networking is a set of computers of any size that are located in a large geographic area. Large-computer processing and Internet computing are not technical computer terms.

35. A: Client/server. Client/server computing is the process in which one computer, the client, provides the processing power, while another computer, the server, provides the data and information for the client. Wide-area networking is a set up of computers of any size that are located in a large geographic area. Large-computer processing and Internet computing are not technical computer terms. Mainframe computers are computers that are set up to take the computer processing load but may be connected to small computers, such as dumb terminals.

36. C: Internal hard drives. Hard drives provide information for the local computer; while they can be shared to be accessed over the local-area network, they are not actually part of the network. Cat-5e cabling is often an important part of the network, as this cabling is used to transmit network signals and communication. RJ-45 jacks are the wall jacks and network interface card (NIC) jacks that are used to connect the Ethernet cables to the different network devices. The NICs are the cards the computers use to convert their network requests into signals. Hubs can be used by the local-area network to provide additional ways to connect more than one device to another.

37. D: Penguin. Penguin is not an operating system, although it is the mascot of the Linux operating system. Windows is the mainstream operating system created by Microsoft and is used on most personal computers (PCs) today. Linux is an open-source operating system that is free to download and install on PCs and servers. Snow Leopard is the operating system used on Apple Macintosh computers. OS/2 is an operating system made by the IBM Corporation.

38. A: An interface between the retailer and the consumer. A computer can be part of the interface between the retailer and the consumer, but an operating system has nothing to do with that process, nor is it associated with transaction processing. Instead, an operating system does serve as the interface between the user and the applications and between the applications and the hardware. The operating system also manages resources for the computer and acts as a host for all computer applications.

39. E: Central processing unit. The central processing unit (CPU) is part of the hardware of the computer. Nearly all CPUs are capable of working with more than one operating system, and the operating systems are written to use the different CPUs. The operating system consists of a kernel, which is the heart of the operating system; system and application programs that are bundled with the operating system; and a system library that contains a number of functions and other library codes that help the operating system function.

40. B: 802.11g. The standard, 802.11g, published by the Institute of Electrical and Electronic Engineers, is used to describe all wireless computer communications. There are others, such as 802.11a, 802.11b, and 802.11n, that describe different speeds of wireless communications. The 802.1 standard is used to describe port-based access control. The 811g, 811.2g, and 811.5g are simply incorrect combinations of the correct standards and have nothing to do with computers or communications.

41. C: Line of sight. Cellular signals cannot curve or bend and, therefore, can only be transmitted when there is a clear line of sight from the cell tower to the cell device. A two-mile limit is not associated with cell signals. Cell signals can suffer from local interference, but this is not a limiting factor in communication signals. The curvature of the earth does not affect cellular signals, except when that affects the line of sight. In general, satellites have nothing to do with cellular signals.

42. C: Cellular phones. Cellular phones require cell signals that are bounced between cellular towers and do not use satellites. Global positioning systems and auto navigation systems are similar devices that cannot work without direct communication with a number of satellites. Satellite phones also work directly with satellites to send and receive their signals. Remote-location television signals also work by receiving their programming and information directly from a geosynchronous satellite.

43. B: Massive. There is no such programming methodology called massive. Scrum is a relatively simple methodology that has only a few rules to assist with agile software development. Extreme programming is a set of best practices that are used in software development and that are taken to extremes. Unified process is an extensible framework that is customized for use in individual companies. Rational unified process is a detailed, commercial, development process owned by the IBM Corporation.

44. E: It works on all platforms and operating systems. In fact, Visual Basic will only work on Microsoft operating systems and cannot function under any other operating system. It is a tool that has been developed to help programmers learn programming, and it is owned by Microsoft. In addition, the Microsoft Visual Basic program, when installed, includes both a compiler and an interpreter.

45. A: Cobol. Cobol is an interpreted language, and programs are executed by using the interpreter so no compiler is required. Pascal, C++, Assembly Language, and Java programs all are written in plain text and then must be sent through a compiler (and in some cases, a linker program) before they are in a form that can be executed by the computer.

46. E: Maintenance. After software has been created and released, the maintenance phase must begin to support the software. Often while in the maintenance phase, the system development life cycle (SDLC) starts over to ensure that the needs of the organization have not changed during the development process. Planning always needs to be done in the first phases of the SDLC. Design must be completed before the programming stage. Testing should always be done before the software is released. Users must be trained, and then the software can go into the maintenance phase.

47. A: It is a sequence of stages where each stage must be completed before starting the next. The waterfall method of the system development life cycle (SDLC) is one of the oldest SDLC methods still used in certain types of application development. A sequence of stages that repeats over and over again until the process is complete describes the spiral method. Steps associated with rapid application development or rapid prototyping involve creating a prototype that works and then developing the software. Dividing the project into parts, building each part separately, and then combining the parts are typical steps of the incremental model of development. A combination of the waterfall method and the spiral method is exemplified by building a proof of concept and then modifying it as needed for the users.

48. D: The waterfall method. The waterfall method is one of the original methods of the system development life cycle and has nothing to do with agile methods. The agile software development methods all attempt to make the repetitions of the development cycle as short as possible and slowly increment new ideas and processes to the development cycle. Examples of different agile software development methods include crystal methods, dynamic systems development model, scrum, and extreme programming.

49. B: Project manager. The project manager is the one person most responsible for the development of the project plan to ensure that the plan is completed. The project team works for the project manager, assisting with the completion of the plan. The project sponsor takes ownership of the project but is not responsible for the actual project plan. The project stakeholders have a vested interest in the outcome of the project, but they do not develop the project plan. The steering committee works with project oversight and control.

50. B: Additional products and services to support the project. The project manager, as part of the project plan, identifies products and services that will help complete the project and can obtain those resources from outside vendors when financially feasible. The primary decision-making for the project lies with the project manager. The user interface decisions are made by a set of customers in combination with developers and team members. Oversight and control of the project is done by the project steering committee. Task and technical leadership is provided by team leaders.

51. D: Server management. Management of servers is usually done by internal groups associated with the hardware or network management. Unless the specific project is developing and installing servers, management of the servers does not fall into the domain of project management. Each project management system, however, must have the ability to keep track of the organizational systems, must be able to manage documents and track time, and must have some way to keep up communications with all the participants in the project.

52. A: Batch processing. Batch processing describes the process in which all data (e.g., all of the deposits for a bank) are collected and then processed, one item at a time, in the order in which they were received. Real-time processing describes the process in which data are input and processed immediately, instead of waiting until all data are received. Interactive and online processing are similar to real-time processing, as the data are processed immediately. Master file processing is not an actual data processing type.

53. B: Real-time processing. Real-time processing ensures that data are processed immediately. In an air-traffic control system, the users of the system need to know where all the aircraft are at every moment. Any delay in the processing would obviously be disastrous. Batch processing is when all the data are collected, one item at a time, and then processed. Interactive and online processing work in a similar manner as real-time processing, but not nearly as quickly, and in the situation described in the question, each second makes a difference.

54. E: Malleability. Malleability is the ability to change and adapt. A transaction in a transaction processing system must be unchangeable once it has been entered into the system. To adjust a transaction in a transaction processing system, another transaction must be entered. A transaction must be atomic; that is, it must be complete in itself. It must be consistent and unchangeable once entered. It must be isolated and not depend on another transaction to complete its actions, and it must be durable and stay in the system once it has been committed.

55. C: Three. The typical computer user can only store and process a certain number of different items at one time. When an application shows just one font on the screen at a time, it is easy to understand and read. The more fonts that are presented at one time, the more complex the application appears to be. With more than three fonts, the user cannot effectively process the different types, and the application effectively becomes unusable.

56. B: Colon. The colon symbol typically appears after a label for a certain type of information that is to be provided to the program. It is often followed by a blank or a text box where the user is expected to type. The single apostrophe has meanings throughout computer science but seldom has any meaning to users. The semicolon has the same function to users as it does in the English language. The exclamation point is often used in computer science to indicate the not operation. The asterisk is widely used as a wildcard character.

57. D: An indication that the letter can be used as an access key. Traditionally in computer application programs, users know that they can use a certain key combination (e.g., alt, app, function) with the underlined letter to access that letter's menu option, label, or text box. This is standard across applications and platforms, so any application that does not follow this standard is hard for a user to use. This process of allowing a keyboard key combination to have a special function in the application software is called an access key.

58. A: Syntax. Syntax refers to the rules regarding what symbols can appear and where they can appear in the source code of a program. When these very strict rules are not followed by the programmer, when the program attempts to run, or when it is compiled, a syntax error is generated by either the interpreter or the compiler. These errors typically are severe errors, and the program will not run (or even compile) when there are even very simple syntax errors in the source code.

59. C: Add 1 to X, and store the value in the variable X. In most programming languages, the logic appears as the reverse to the human reader. To a human, reading this line from left to right makes no logical sense. However, in most programming languages, the line is processed in order of precedence. In this case, the program first determines the value that is stored in the variable location that is named X, and then the value of one is added to that value; the instruction of the equals sign (called the assignment operator) follows, assigning the result of the summation to the variable location called X.

60. C: It is an example of sample instructions that are written to help write actual source codes. A pseudocode is written when a programmer attempts to determine how the code will work and how the code will fit with other codes. There are no rules to writing pseudocodes, and each programmer's pseudocode is likely to be different from anyone else's pseudocode. After working through the process of determining how the code works and writing the pseudocode, the programmer can use the pseudocode to write the actual source codes, no matter what programming language is used.

61. E: BUT. Logical operators are those that take one or two operands, perform their operation, and return a result of either true or false. Some logical operators are binary and require two operands; AND, OR, and XOR are all binary. The NOT logical operator is a unary operator and only requires one operand. In that case, the NOT operation returns the opposite of the operand. The word BUT is a conjunction in the English language; it is not used in computer languages.

62. D: When A is 10 and B is 10. This problem has two conditional statements, and each statement has a true and a false section. If the value of A is less than 6, then the code will move to the "print goodbye" section and never see, read, or process the conditional statement with the B. If the value of A is greater than 6, the code will continue inside the true portion of the statement and will execute the conditional with the B portion. If the value of B is less than 7, the code will execute the "print nothing" line. In all other cases, the code will continue to the "print hello" line. Therefore, any time that A is larger than 6 and B is not less than 7, the code will execute the "print hello" line.

63. D: 11. In the binary numbering system, the only possible digits that can be used are 0 and 1. No other digits will fit in the binary number system at any time. In this same system, the first digit represents one item. The second digit represents the twos column. When presented with 1 + 1 + 1, the calculation can be done in base 10, resulting in 3, and then the 3 can be converted into binary. In that case, a 1 in the ones digit plus a 1 in the twos digit equals 3 (1*1 + 1*2). The result can also be obtained by using only binary: adding 1 and 1 results in a 0, carrying the 1 to the two's digit (10). Adding one more will result in a 1 in the one's digit as well (11).

64. A: A blueprint of an item. A class describes how an item is stored but is incapable of actually storing any information or data. The variable cannot be the class, because the class just describes the object that is created. Classes do not take up locations in memory because they are just plans. A class cannot contain values, so it cannot store the value of true or false.

65. A: Constructor. Any function that automatically is executed simply by the creation of an object of that class is called a constructor function. Usually these functions have the same name as the class and are used to initialize member variables for the object. Mutator functions are functions that are designed to change the contents of member variables, usually based on rules combined with user or function input. Initial, first, and instantiated are class functions.

66. B: Has different behavior, depending on the input to the function. A polymorphic function can be "called," using a different number and type of parameter but with the same function name. All functions that are nonpolymorphic have one matching set of parameters, and all function calls must use this exact number, type, and order of parameters or the function will not be "called." Polymorphic functions allow the user more flexibility when designing and writing a computer application program.

67. C: The amount of memory reserved. When a data type is defined in a programming language, either with an interpreted language or a compiled language, the primary purpose is to define the amount of available memory. This memory is used by the variable of the specific type; if a value is too large for a memory location, there will be an overflow of some sort, depending on the programming language and the compiler or interpreter.

68. D: More than one type of data. Structures are normally used to store information about an entity that contains more than one type of data structure (e.g., storing information about classes that have names, titles, credit hours, lab fees). Because these data are different, they require different amounts of space in memory. Storing them in a data type that is large enough for all of them but that is not a structure uses more memory than is necessary.

69. A: Instantiation. Instantiating a variable is asking the program or operating system to reserve a certain amount of space (determined by the data type) in memory for the variable. Depending on the program language, the process of instantiating may or may not also initialize the variable and store a certain default value in that location. Some languages also refer to this process as dimensioning a variable.

70. B: A compact disc player. A random access file can access any portion of the file at any time, simply by knowing which of the records is needed; the records are all the same size, so determining the location of the specific file is as simple as multiplying the size of the record by the record number desired. This allows the program to read any file in any order at any time, much like a compact disc (CD) player allows users to skip songs they do not like to listen to any song on the CD in any order.

71. B: It helps determine which program should open the file. The primary purpose of the file extension is to tell the operating system which application program should be opened to display a given file, particularly when a file is not accessed through its application program. While the file extension is often set by the program that created the file, a number of different programs can save files with different file names or even the same file extension. The user of most operating systems can set up these options.

72. A: The entire file will be read every time it is accessed. A flat file must be accessed sequentially, and the entire file must be read from start to finish, even if only one record from the file is desired. There is also no way, when using a sequential access file, to back up through the records. If a record is missed, the file must be processed again from the start. The sequential access file has no major effect on the space used on a hard drive, so all answers related to the amount of space or size of the file are incorrect.

73. A: A disc storage system. A disc storage system is typically required by a database management system, but the management and storage of that system is determine by the operating system of the computer and is simply used by the database management system. A database management system, however, primarily consists of a modeling language, data structures, query language, and some sort of transaction mechanism.

74. B: Transferring. There is no database called a transferring database. A relational database links information in tables with common key fields to ensure data are accurate and stored efficiently. An object-oriented database is similar to a relational database, but information is stored in terms of classes and objects instead of fields and tables. An online analytical process database is used for viewing data, not making changes to it. A flat-file database has no tables but stores all the information in one large string or a large file. These are typically used for storing very small amounts of information.

75. C: Debian Linux. Debian Linux is a type of operating system and has nothing to do with databases or database management systems. Microsoft Access, a database management system produced by Microsoft, is designed for ease of use and for small database applications. The database management system designed and sold by IBM is IBM DB2. An open-source database management system, MySQL, is often used with the Internet and web-enabled applications. Oracle is the relational database management system created by the Oracle Company.

76. B: Column names. In an SQL statement, the information following the select keyword includes the number of columns that will appear in the result and aliases for those columns, if required. The table names are listed in the "from" clause, not the "select" clause. In database systems, there is no such thing as "row numbers." The number of rows to be returned is determined by the information in the "where" clause of the SQL statement.

77. D: Three. In the example given in the question, there are five records in the table. The select statement requests just the ID number, or column, to be displayed in the result set. The SQL statement requests all rows, or records, where the contents of the department field start with the number 16, followed by any other symbol or character. In the example given in the question, there are three records that meet that criterion: the first two records that have a department number of 16A and the fourth record that has a department number of 16B.

78. C: Where. The "where" clause limits the number of rows returned in the result set; this limitation is based on the requirements placed on the data in the fields and on the requirement that data are found in other tables, using the "join" statement or just equals signs based on different fields in different tables. The "select" statement can only contain columns that are to appear in the results. The "from" clause can only contain a list of tables that contain the data to be analyzed. The "order by" clause will not affect the number of rows, just the order in which they appear when the result set is displayed. There is no such section as the "table join" in standard SQL.

79. A: HTML. Hypertext markup language, or HTML, has been used since the beginning of the Internet to communicate and display web pages. All web browsers can understand and interpret HTML markup. An extension of HTML is known as XML and is not a basic language of the web. An expanded version of HTML and XML is XHTML that is understood by some, but not all, of the most current browsers, and no older web browsers. A dynamic HTML language is DHTML that makes web pages more flexible, but it is not understood by all browsers. The final acronym, TMLH, is not at all related to the Internet or the web.

80. A: DHTML. A dynamic hypertext markup language, or DHTML, is a hypertext language that was created to make web pages more dynamic and changeable. It is recognized and used by most current web browsers. Visual Basic is a programming language that is primarily used to teach programming students basic computer programming. The W3C is the world wide web consortium, a group that is charged with maintaining and defining standards for the Internet and the world wide web. A simple hypertext markup language, or HTML, can only create state web pages. Apache is a web server technology used to host and serve web pages over a network.

81. D: Assembly language. Assembly language is used to communicate at the lowest levels of a computer, often directly to the processor and the registers of the processor. It is not used with any web page or Internet technology, as it is also processor-dependent where the Internet is not. An open-source preprocessor programming language, or PHP, is used to create dynamic web pages and access databases. JavaScript is a scripting language that is used to make a page more interactive or to create special effects on a web page. The processing language used by Microsoft, or ASP, is used when creating Microsoft server-based web pages. Cold fusion is another web preprocessing language that is used to access databases and make the web pages more dynamic.

82. E: Storage. When setting up or running a data mining system, the data mining system must, at the least, be capable of classification, clustering, learning rules, and regression analysis. The data mining system itself is not concerned with the storage of data, only searching through the data for analytical purposes.

83. A: Wedding planning. Wedding planning, while on some levels a complex task, has a very small amount of data associated with it. Even the most extensive wedding plan, such as inviting hundreds of guests to the wedding, does not require data warehousing. Data warehousing is for storage of massive amounts of data; for example, credit card analysis involves millions of transactions and records, which can make use of data warehousing. Any application that has a large amount of data, such as insurance records, federal law enforcement, and help desk calls may benefit from data warehousing.

84. E: Final score of the Saints–Dolphins game on Sunday. Data mining is designed to read large amounts of data, searching for patterns that are driven by certain events. These patterns can then be applied to future events to determine an estimated outcome or a probability of that outcome. This can be seen in sales amounts of items at certain locations. Data mining can determine factual or historical data, such as the total number of books sold at a certain location. However, data mining cannot accurately predict the results of a game based on chance with as many variables as a football game.

85. E: None. The United States Constitution does not guarantee the right to privacy. Instead, the claimed right to privacy is based on various court decisions and federal laws. The right to privacy, especially when applied to computers, is a very weak right, and in the case of the Internet, courts have ruled that most people cannot expect privacy at all.

86. A: SSL. Secure socket layers, or SSL, is a method of encryption; SSL attempts to secure data in transmission by encrypting it before sending, relying on the receiver to decrypt the information. Hypertext markup language, or HTML, is a plain text language used for web pages; HTML is not at all secure. A programming language, or PHP, is used on the web; PHP is used to develop dynamic web pages. Time to live, or TTL is a measurement of time; TTL is concerned with web servers and delay times in network communications. As an Internet service provider, ISP is the company that provides access to the Internet for individuals and companies.

87. B: It's a small file on your computer disc. Cookies are small files that are used by web pages to track information about you when you accessed certain web sites. The files are generally harmless and store information about your last visit to a specific web site. For example, a cookie might store your user name so that you do not have to log onto a web site a second time in the same day. Generally, cookies only work and are set by individual sites, but in certain circumstances, you can enable cookies to track information and data from one site to another web site.

88. C: It has no secret code and can be modified by the user. Open-source software may be developed by one individual or many individuals. What makes the software open source is that the individuals release the source of the work to the world and will allow individuals who follow some simple guidelines access to the code. Anyone can see how the code works and can modify any part of the code for their own needs. To be truly open-source software, the software also can be modified and distributed at no charge to others.

89. D: Microsoft Office. By definition, open-source software must have its source code available to the public to be viewed and modified. The source code for the Microsoft software is a very closely guarded corporate secret that will never be sold to the public, much less released for free. Open Office is an open-source productivity suite that rivals Microsoft Office. Apache is the world's most popular web server software that is completely open source. Tomcat is an open-source example of software that can be used with a web server to process Java and other programming languages. Linux is a complete operating system that is entirely open source.

90. A: Copyright laws. Copyright laws protect any author of any work that is created. They are typically applied to musical scores and written work, but they also apply to computer programs. The copyright is created as soon as the program is saved. Patents are used to protect physical inventions created by individuals or corporations. Trademarks are used to protect certain symbols, drawings, or sayings associated with a specific product or service. Service marks are used in some countries to protect symbols associated with services, much like trademarks. Privacy laws have nothing to do with the protection of computer software.

91. C: Designing work system layouts to conform to the human body. Ergonomics is the study of designing chairs, keyboards, desks, and other computer equipment to work with the human body in ways that will reduce potential stress or repetitive movement injuries. Chairs that are specially designed to be comfortable and effective result from the study of ergonomics. All devices made to reduce or eliminate carpal tunnel injuries are also part of the study of ergonomics.

92. E: Wrists. The carpal tunnel is a section of the wrist through which a number of tendons pass. These tendons are attached to the muscles in the arms and the bones in the wrist, and when you move your fingers, these muscles and tendons are what cause them to move. When you are typing on a keyboard, the forearm muscles pull these tendons. With repeated use at poor angles, these tendons can become irritated and swell, pressing on the median nerve and causing carpal tunnel syndrome.

93. B: Using computers to work from home or other remote locations. Telecommuting is when a worker works in a location other than the office, usually at home. Many of these positions are in technology; the telecommuting worker often uses a computer that is connected to the computer system at the place of employment and often participates in conference calls and other forms of nonphysical contact with other employees.

94. D: Technical information in nontechnical terms. A technical writer is usually employed by a technical company but has an English degree or experience in writing. These writers take complex technical information and write the information in a manner that nontechnical people can understand. For example, technical writers often write instruction manuals for consumers or help files, without knowing the technical details of how the programs and applications work.

95. A: Recording and storing evidence for law enforcement agencies. A computer forensic technician is a person who has experience and knowledge of computers, computer technology, networks, and also law enforcement procedures. These technicians work with computers that have been seized for criminal evidence. Hard drives may contain evidence that can be used in criminal prosecutions, and computer forensic technicians are skilled enough to be able retrieve data from the computers that can be presented in a courtroom.

96. B: They require a great deal of experience and training. Computer technical support positions are often entry-level positions, allowing many people to start a career in computer technologies. A+ certification can show the employer that the individual has the knowledge and ability to perform basic computer support positions, as this test asks questions about basic computer knowledge. There are many different types and levels of support positions. Often the least experienced support technician is assigned to level 1 support, and when problems occur that are too difficult for that level of support, the problem is bumped to the next level with more experienced support technicians.

97. C: Antivirus program. A malicious program that attempts to do damage to a computer is a virus program. These come from various sources but reach personal computers through network connections. An antivirus program remains active on a computer and attempts to stop all viruses from attacking the computer. Virus and spyware programs are programs that attempt to do damage to a computer, which is the opposite of an antivirus program. An application program is any program on your computer that completes any task. An e-mail program is more likely to spawn and release a virus than protect your computer from a virus.

98. D: Opening e-mail attachments. Billions of e-mail messages are transmitted every day, and many contain viruses. The most common way for a virus to spread is when a person opens an e-mail attachment that contains a virus, not knowing that there is a virus in the attachment. Open-network connections typically require active attacks and, therefore, are just not as common as sending e-mails. Holes in firewalls allow individuals (or robots) access to computers but are not usually used to spread viruses. Sharing discs is a very powerful and quick way to spread viruses, but with the prevalence of networks, sharing discs and drives is not as common as e-mails. Internet web browsers can spread viruses, but only if the user has the security settings on low and they give permission to the attacking program, which is uncommon.

99. E: When a person steals information about another and uses that information fraudulently. Identify theft can be performed using a computer, but it is most often accomplished by stealing receipts and other information from trash bins. Securing data on a computer is a way to prevent identity theft. Losing a driver's license may lead to identity theft, but simply losing it does not cause identity theft. A program that attacks a computer is a virus, not identity theft. Stolen passwords and user identifications is simply theft; if these, in turn, are used to access a personal account, that is fraud not identity theft.

100. B: Buying office supplies from the local office supply company. Buying supplies is a normal process of doing business. Outsourcing is contracting with another person or another company to do business to complete your own business. Buying any type of material or software is a type of outsourcing, even if it does not go outside a company. Having sections of computer codes written by programmers who can provide it cheaper is a common type of outsourcing in computer companies. Using prewritten software is also a common way to outsource a task.

How to Overcome Test Anxiety

Just the thought of taking a test is enough to make most people a little nervous. A test is an important event that can have a long-term impact on your future, so it's important to take it seriously and it's natural to feel anxious about performing well. But just because anxiety is normal, that doesn't mean that it's helpful in test taking, or that you should simply accept it as part of your life. Anxiety can have a variety of effects. These effects can be mild, like making you feel slightly nervous, or severe, like blocking your ability to focus or remember even a simple detail.

If you experience test anxiety—whether severe or mild—it's important to know how to beat it. To discover this, first you need to understand what causes test anxiety.

Causes of Test Anxiety

While we often think of anxiety as an uncontrollable emotional state, it can actually be caused by simple, practical things. One of the most common causes of test anxiety is that a person does not feel adequately prepared for their test. This feeling can be the result of many different issues such as poor study habits or lack of organization, but the most common culprit is time management. Starting to study too late, failing to organize your study time to cover all of the material, or being distracted while you study will mean that you're not well prepared for the test. This may lead to cramming the night before, which will cause you to be physically and mentally exhausted for the test. Poor time management also contributes to feelings of stress, fear, and hopelessness as you realize you are not well prepared but don't know what to do about it.

Other times, test anxiety is not related to your preparation for the test but comes from unresolved fear. This may be a past failure on a test, or poor performance on tests in general. It may come from comparing yourself to others who seem to be performing better or from the stress of living up to expectations. Anxiety may be driven by fears of the future—how failure on this test would affect your educational and career goals. These fears are often completely irrational, but they can still negatively impact your test performance.

Elements of Test Anxiety

As mentioned earlier, test anxiety is considered to be an emotional state, but it has physical and mental components as well. Sometimes you may not even realize that you are suffering from test anxiety until you notice the physical symptoms. These can include trembling hands, rapid heartbeat, sweating, nausea, and tense muscles. Extreme anxiety may lead to fainting or vomiting. Obviously, any of these symptoms can have a negative impact on testing. It is important to recognize them as soon as they begin to occur so that you can address the problem before it damages your performance.

The mental components of test anxiety include trouble focusing and inability to remember learned information. During a test, your mind is on high alert, which can help you recall information and stay focused for an extended period of time. However, anxiety interferes with your mind's natural processes, causing you to blank out, even on the questions you know well. The strain of testing during anxiety makes it difficult to stay focused, especially on a test that may take several hours. Extreme anxiety can take a huge mental toll, making it difficult not only to recall test information but even to understand the test questions or pull your thoughts together.

Effects of Test Anxiety

Test anxiety is like a disease—if left untreated, it will get progressively worse. Anxiety leads to poor performance, and this reinforces the feelings of fear and failure, which in turn lead to poor performances on subsequent tests. It can grow from a mild nervousness to a crippling condition. If allowed to progress, test anxiety can have a big impact on your schooling, and consequently on your future.

Test anxiety can spread to other parts of your life. Anxiety on tests can become anxiety in any stressful situation, and blanking on a test can turn into panicking in a job situation. But fortunately, you don't have to let anxiety rule your testing and determine your grades. There are a number of relatively simple steps you can take to move past anxiety and function normally on a test and in the rest of life.

Physical Steps for Beating Test Anxiety

While test anxiety is a serious problem, the good news is that it can be overcome. It doesn't have to control your ability to think and remember information. While it may take time, you can begin taking steps today to beat anxiety.

Just as your first hint that you may be struggling with anxiety comes from the physical symptoms, the first step to treating it is also physical. Rest is crucial for having a clear, strong mind. If you are tired, it is much easier to give in to anxiety. But if you establish good sleep habits, your body and mind will be ready to perform optimally, without the strain of exhaustion. Additionally, sleeping well helps you to retain information better, so you're more likely to recall the answers when you see the test questions.

Getting good sleep means more than going to bed on time. It's important to allow your brain time to relax. Take study breaks from time to time so it doesn't get overworked, and don't study right before bed. Take time to rest your mind before trying to rest your body, or you may find it difficult to fall asleep.

Along with sleep, other aspects of physical health are important in preparing for a test. Good nutrition is vital for good brain function. Sugary foods and drinks may give a burst of energy but this burst is followed by a crash, both physically and emotionally. Instead, fuel your body with protein and vitamin-rich foods.

Also, drink plenty of water. Dehydration can lead to headaches and exhaustion, especially if your brain is already under stress from the rigors of the test. Particularly if your test is a long one, drink water during the breaks. And if possible, take an energy-boosting snack to eat between sections.

Along with sleep and diet, a third important part of physical health is exercise. Maintaining a steady workout schedule is helpful, but even taking 5-minute study breaks to walk can help get your blood pumping faster and clear your head. Exercise also releases endorphins, which contribute to a positive feeling and can help combat test anxiety.

When you nurture your physical health, you are also contributing to your mental health. If your body is healthy, your mind is much more likely to be healthy as well. So take time to rest, nourish your body with healthy food and water, and get moving as much as possible. Taking these physical steps will make you stronger and more able to take the mental steps necessary to overcome test anxiety.

Mental Steps for Beating Test Anxiety

Working on the mental side of test anxiety can be more challenging, but as with the physical side, there are clear steps you can take to overcome it. As mentioned earlier, test anxiety often stems from lack of preparation, so the obvious solution is to prepare for the test. Effective studying may be the most important weapon you have for beating test anxiety, but you can and should employ several other mental tools to combat fear.

First, boost your confidence by reminding yourself of past success—tests or projects that you aced. If you're putting as much effort into preparing for this test as you did for those, there's no reason you should expect to fail here. Work hard to prepare; then trust your preparation.

Second, surround yourself with encouraging people. It can be helpful to find a study group, but be sure that the people you're around will encourage a positive attitude. If you spend time with others who are anxious or cynical, this will only contribute to your own anxiety. Look for others who are motivated to study hard from a desire to succeed, not from a fear of failure.

Third, reward yourself. A test is physically and mentally tiring, even without anxiety, and it can be helpful to have something to look forward to. Plan an activity following the test, regardless of the outcome, such as going to a movie or getting ice cream.

When you are taking the test, if you find yourself beginning to feel anxious, remind yourself that you know the material. Visualize successfully completing the test. Then take a few deep, relaxing breaths and return to it. Work through the questions carefully but with confidence, knowing that you are capable of succeeding.

Developing a healthy mental approach to test taking will also aid in other areas of life. Test anxiety affects more than just the actual test—it can be damaging to your mental health and even contribute to depression. It's important to beat test anxiety before it becomes a problem for more than testing.

Study Strategy

Being prepared for the test is necessary to combat anxiety, but what does being prepared look like? You may study for hours on end and still not feel prepared. What you need is a strategy for test prep. The next few pages outline our recommended steps to help you plan out and conquer the challenge of preparation.

Step 1: Scope Out the Test

Learn everything you can about the format (multiple choice, essay, etc.) and what will be on the test. Gather any study materials, course outlines, or sample exams that may be available. Not only will this help you to prepare, but knowing what to expect can help to alleviate test anxiety.

Step 2: Map Out the Material

Look through the textbook or study guide and make note of how many chapters or sections it has. Then divide these over the time you have. For example, if a book has 15 chapters and you have five days to study, you need to cover three chapters each day. Even better, if you have the time, leave an extra day at the end for overall review after you have gone through the material in depth.

If time is limited, you may need to prioritize the material. Look through it and make note of which sections you think you already have a good grasp on, and which need review. While you are studying, skim quickly through the familiar sections and take more time on the challenging parts.

Write out your plan so you don't get lost as you go. Having a written plan also helps you feel more in control of the study, so anxiety is less likely to arise from feeling overwhelmed at the amount to cover.

Step 3: Gather Your Tools

Decide what study method works best for you. Do you prefer to highlight in the book as you study and then go back over the highlighted portions? Or do you type out notes of the important information? Or is it helpful to make flashcards that you can carry with you? Assemble the pens, index cards, highlighters, post-it notes, and any other materials you may need so you won't be distracted by getting up to find things while you study.

If you're having a hard time retaining the information or organizing your notes, experiment with different methods. For example, try color-coding by subject with colored pens, highlighters, or post-it notes. If you learn better by hearing, try recording yourself reading your notes so you can listen while in the car, working out, or simply sitting at your desk. Ask a friend to quiz you from your flashcards, or try teaching someone the material to solidify it in your mind.

Step 4: Create Your Environment

It's important to avoid distractions while you study. This includes both the obvious distractions like visitors and the subtle distractions like an uncomfortable chair (or a too-comfortable couch that makes you want to fall asleep). Set up the best study environment possible: good lighting and a comfortable work area. If background music helps you focus, you may want to turn it on, but otherwise keep the room quiet. If you are using a computer to take notes, be sure you don't have any other windows open, especially applications like social media, games, or anything else that could distract you. Silence your phone and turn off notifications. Be sure to keep water close by so you stay hydrated while you study (but avoid unhealthy drinks and snacks).

Also, take into account the best time of day to study. Are you freshest first thing in the morning? Try to set aside some time then to work through the material. Is your mind clearer in the afternoon or evening? Schedule your study session then. Another method is to study at the same time of day that you will take the test, so that your brain gets used to working on the material at that time and will be ready to focus at test time.

Step 5: Study!

Once you have done all the study preparation, it's time to settle into the actual studying. Sit down, take a few moments to settle your mind so you can focus, and begin to follow your study plan. Don't give in to distractions or let yourself procrastinate. This is your time to prepare so you'll be ready to fearlessly approach the test. Make the most of the time and stay focused.

Of course, you don't want to burn out. If you study too long you may find that you're not retaining the information very well. Take regular study breaks. For example, taking five minutes out of every hour to walk briskly, breathing deeply and swinging your arms, can help your mind stay fresh.

As you get to the end of each chapter or section, it's a good idea to do a quick review. Remind yourself of what you learned and work on any difficult parts. When you feel that you've mastered the material, move on to the next part. At the end of your study session, briefly skim through your notes again.

But while review is helpful, cramming last minute is NOT. If at all possible, work ahead so that you won't need to fit all your study into the last day. Cramming overloads your brain with more information than it can process and retain, and your tired mind may struggle to recall even previously learned information when it is overwhelmed with last-minute study. Also, the urgent nature of cramming and the stress placed on your brain contribute to anxiety. You'll be more likely to go to the test feeling unprepared and having trouble thinking clearly.

So don't cram, and don't stay up late before the test, even just to review your notes at a leisurely pace. Your brain needs rest more than it needs to go over the information again. In fact, plan to finish your studies by noon or early afternoon the day before the test. Give your brain the rest of the day to relax or focus on other things, and get a good night's sleep. Then you will be fresh for the test and better able to recall what you've studied.

STEP 6: TAKE A PRACTICE TEST

Many courses offer sample tests, either online or in the study materials. This is an excellent resource to check whether you have mastered the material, as well as to prepare for the test format and environment.

Check the test format ahead of time: the number of questions, the type (multiple choice, free response, etc.), and the time limit. Then create a plan for working through them. For example, if you have 30 minutes to take a 60-question test, your limit is 30 seconds per question. Spend less time on the questions you know well so that you can take more time on the difficult ones.

If you have time to take several practice tests, take the first one open book, with no time limit. Work through the questions at your own pace and make sure you fully understand them. Gradually work up to taking a test under test conditions: sit at a desk with all study materials put away and set a timer. Pace yourself to make sure you finish the test with time to spare and go back to check your answers if you have time.

After each test, check your answers. On the questions you missed, be sure you understand why you missed them. Did you misread the question (tests can use tricky wording)? Did you forget the information? Or was it something you hadn't learned? Go back and study any shaky areas that the practice tests reveal.

Taking these tests not only helps with your grade, but also aids in combating test anxiety. If you're already used to the test conditions, you're less likely to worry about it, and working through tests until you're scoring well gives you a confidence boost. Go through the practice tests until you feel comfortable, and then you can go into the test knowing that you're ready for it.

Test Tips

On test day, you should be confident, knowing that you've prepared well and are ready to answer the questions. But aside from preparation, there are several test day strategies you can employ to maximize your performance.

First, as stated before, get a good night's sleep the night before the test (and for several nights before that, if possible). Go into the test with a fresh, alert mind rather than staying up late to study.

Try not to change too much about your normal routine on the day of the test. It's important to eat a nutritious breakfast, but if you normally don't eat breakfast at all, consider eating just a protein bar. If you're a coffee drinker, go ahead and have your normal coffee. Just make sure you time it so that the caffeine doesn't wear off right in the middle of your test. Avoid sugary beverages, and drink enough water to stay hydrated but not so much that you need a restroom break 10 minutes into the test. If your test isn't first thing in the morning, consider going for a walk or doing a light workout before the test to get your blood flowing.

Allow yourself enough time to get ready, and leave for the test with plenty of time to spare so you won't have the anxiety of scrambling to arrive in time. Another reason to be early is to select a good seat. It's helpful to sit away from doors and windows, which can be distracting. Find a good seat, get out your supplies, and settle your mind before the test begins.

When the test begins, start by going over the instructions carefully, even if you already know what to expect. Make sure you avoid any careless mistakes by following the directions.

Then begin working through the questions, pacing yourself as you've practiced. If you're not sure on an answer, don't spend too much time on it, and don't let it shake your confidence. Either skip it and come back later, or eliminate as many wrong answers as possible and guess among the remaining ones. Don't dwell on these questions as you continue—put them out of your mind and focus on what lies ahead.

Be sure to read all of the answer choices, even if you're sure the first one is the right answer. Sometimes you'll find a better one if you keep reading. But don't second-guess yourself if you do immediately know the answer. Your gut instinct is usually right. Don't let test anxiety rob you of the information you know.

If you have time at the end of the test (and if the test format allows), go back and review your answers. Be cautious about changing any, since your first instinct tends to be correct, but make sure you didn't misread any of the questions or accidentally mark the wrong answer choice. Look over any you skipped and make an educated guess.

At the end, leave the test feeling confident. You've done your best, so don't waste time worrying about your performance or wishing you could change anything. Instead, celebrate the successful completion of this test. And finally, use this test to learn how to deal with anxiety even better next time.

Review Video: Test Anxiety
Visit mometrix.com/academy and enter code: 100340

Important Qualification

Not all anxiety is created equal. If your test anxiety is causing major issues in your life beyond the classroom or testing center, or if you are experiencing troubling physical symptoms related to your anxiety, it may be a sign of a serious physiological or psychological condition. If this sounds like your situation, we strongly encourage you to seek professional help.

Online Resources

Due to our efforts to try to keep this book to a manageable length, we've created a link that will give you access to all of your online resources:

mometrix.com/resources719/clepinfosca

It's Your Moment, Let's Celebrate It!

Share your story @mometrixtestpreparation